PRESIDENTIAL TELEVISION

THE TWENTIETH CENTURY FUND, founded in 1919, and endowed by Edward A. Filene, devotes the major share of its resources to research, concentrating on objective and critical studies of major economic, political, and social issues and institutions. It publishes the results of its research. The Fund attempts to ensure the scholarly quality of works appearing under its imprint; the Trustees and the staff, however, accord authors complete freedom in the statement of opinion and in the interpretation of fact.

PRESIDENTIAL TELEVISION

Newton N. Minow

John Bartlow Martin

Lee M. Mitchell

A TWENTIETH CENTURY FUND REPORT

BASIC BOOKS, INC., *Publishers* NEW YORK

CONTENTS

FOREWORD

THE WORD *Watergate* HARDLY APPEARS IN THIS BOOK, yet it permeates every line. Were there not this comprehensive report on presidential television, the burglary of June 16, 1972 and the virulent infection it identified in our political system would have necessitated such a study. Television is a miracle that American society has never learned to manage and, in its relationship to politics, it has been permitted to run wild. In the case of presidential politics, it has been the means for a corruption of power that has brought the nation to the edge of disgrace. While the Watergate scandal seethed under a Republican administration, it might just as well have plagued a Democratic incumbency.

The drafters of the American Constitution strove diligently to prevent the power of the president from becoming a monopoly, but our inability to manage television has allowed the medium to be converted into an electronic throne.

No mighty king, no ambitious emperor, no pope, or prophet ever dreamt of such an awesome pulpit, so potent a magic wand. In the American experiment with its delicate checks and balances, this device permits the First Amendment and the very heart of the Constitution to be breached, as it bestows on one politician a weapon denied to all others. Free speech and access to the voter presuppose equal tools. Washington and Lincoln could reach crowds no farther than the reach of their voices. True, the telegraph key and then megaphones, wireless, and amplifying systems altered that condition slightly. Coolidge and Hoover never really learned how to use radio and remained its victims. Roosevelt mastered it, as this book recounts, but restraints, including the comparatively low cost of air time, insured its availability to others. It seems almost like ancient history, but in those pioneer days there was something called *sustaining* (noncommercial) *time,* permitting all manner of prime-time access for politicians to debate vital issues.

Television changed all that. At best the wizardry of radio had been an artery of audio communication which sent a voice into the living room. Television was a comprehensive transportation which carried the viewer to the convention floor, to the Vietnam battlefield, to the face of the moon, and to the White House, wherever the camera was directed.

The president, in his ability to command the national attention, diminished the power of all other politicians and, in the case of Richard Nixon, fostered a distortion of our system of safeguards. The impact of television air time and its exorbitant cost provide the chief executive with a monopoly on an instrument only an incumbent president could afford during his campaigns. But in the recent election, all those surplus funds and the resultant overkill made possible the dirty tricks and spying many candidates could not begin to consider, even if their sense of morality so persuaded them. The unique advantage of the president also makes possible the acquisition of air time virtually on request on all three major networks simultaneously. Nixon has commanded and received more free time than any of his predecessors. The not-so-subtle advantage of dominating all three major stations in a single community permits the chief executive to reduce the viewer's alternatives by geometric proportions.

In his first eighteen months in office, President Nixon appeared on prime-time television as many times as the *combined* appearances of Presidents Eisenhower, Kennedy, and Johnson in their first eighteen months in office. During his first forty months in office prior to his Moscow trip, President Nixon had made thirty-two special appearances in prime time, compared to only twenty-four by President Johnson in over five years, ten by President Kennedy in under three years, and twenty-three by President Eisenhower in eight years. These startling figures were prepared by Richard Salant, president of CBS News, in a report in which he concluded that the Nixon incumbency, "representing less than *one-sixth* of the entire period since President Eisenhower's inaugural . . . has accounted for more than *one-third* of these special appearances."

Because President Nixon had so much television time on his own terms, he was able to forsake the hurly-burly risks of the news conference. In his three terms and one month in office, Franklin Delano Roosevelt held 998 presidential news conferences; Truman, 324 in under eight years; Eisenhower, 193 in eight years; Kennedy, 64 in three years; Johnson, 126 in six years; and Richard Nixon, in his first four years, only 28. In the last two years, Nixon permitted only 10. The trend is obvious. Nixon feels it is unnecessary to permit that unruly White House press corps to ask all those tough "have you stopped beating your wife" questions when he can have more time on his own terms. Few kings ever had it so good!

The hidden trap in this procedure was that it placed the president in an isolation booth. Indeed, it can be argued that the commander-in-chief lost contact with the American mood on Watergate, Vietnam, inflation, and his own role in these major issues because he consumed only a controlled diet of information prepared by his own kept corps of in-house journalists who selected and digested the news for him. However, a few sessions with such "pesty" Washington correspondents as Peter Lisagor, Dan Rather, or Lou Cannon at the time of Watergate might have saved the chief executive some of the humiliation in front of Judge Sirica and the Ervin Committee.

The highest price the nation has paid in the misuse of presidential television time is that it denies us all the open ventilation of national issues. The Minow-Martin-Mitchell study examines the historical reasons for this flaw in our system and makes some crucial recommendations. All are constructive and worthy; some, obviously, are easier to describe than to achieve.

Crucial factors in these recommendations are the issues of television access and cost. Because it is not a true parliamentary system, our form of government generates constant questions as to who represents the "loyal opposition" in the ranks of Congress and the party out of office. Who answers the president of the United States when his opposition may be as diverse as George McGovern or George Wallace, or, at another time in history, Charles Percy or John Connally? A multifarious opposition, far from the easy television access enjoyed by the president, finds itself at a grave disadvantage, one which ultimately threatens our democracy.

In these recommendations, there is also the hidden agenda item of the cost of air time. The present system gives the chief executive free air time for messages of State and, by presidential definition, that means virtually every speech he makes excepting some in election years. The latter are funded by the political parties, and that has brought us to the sorry mess we call *Watergate*.

Ours is the only major nation allowing the sale of television time to political parties and office seekers. The tremendous price at which it is sold places candidates in a hole from which they clamber only with the aid of corporations, industry lobbies, and unions. Funds from special interest groups often carry a hidden price tag, one that is ultimately paid by the public.

The inevitable excesses of campaign funding cry out for reform, as even President Nixon has suggested. In 1969, a Twentieth Century Fund commission proposed that all networks simultaneously provide free prime time to presidential nominees and their running mates. The federal government would pay the tab for this "voters' time" based on favored rates. Others have suggested that the broadcast industry provide free time for all candidates as part of their commitment to public service.

In the absence of serious campaign-spending reforms over the last four years, Watergate now spills forth some expensive lessons, many of which are examined and their solutions charted in this study. If our elections are not going to be rigged and our important issues not determined by contributions from dairy and oil lobbies, these issues must be argued on public platforms that politicians can neither control, manage, nor buy.

John Bartlow Martin, one of the superb investigative reporters of the forties and fifties; Newton Minow, former FCC chairman who understood that his task was to regulate the industry, not to serve it; and Lee Mitchell, scholar of the special link between law and the politics of television, have fashioned a primer that can start us down the complex road to reform. This study, however, is neither a miracle nor a mirage. The politicians in Congress and the Federal Communications Commission, and the journalists who report on them, are going to have to work harder than they ever have before in untangling the thicket where, paradoxically, the electromagnetic spectrum and the First Amendment seem to frustrate the method by which this nation makes its decisions. This book identifies and begins to clear that thicket.

FRED W. FRIENDLY

ACKNOWLEDGMENTS

WE THANK THE TWENTIETH CENTURY FUND, and especially M. J. Rossant, for encouragement and support of our study. We are grateful to many people for essential contributions to our research, analysis, and preparation of the manuscript. In particular, we wish to acknowledge our debt to the following people:

1. Ellen M. McGinty, our Research Associate, for indispensable assistance in planning, researching, interviewing, and writing during all phases of the project.

2. Beverly Goldberg, Judith Jacobson, Richard Rust, and Lee Sigal of the staff of The Twentieth Century Fund for constructive comments on early drafts and for editorial and administrative assistance.

3. Stephen Frankel and Jack Fuller for research into the relationship between mass media and the Supreme Court.

4. Helen Hanson, Sheila Hoote, Kathy Strasser, and Millie Wheat for typing, assembling, and keeping track of the many drafts.

We would also like to thank the following people for consenting to be interviewed and discussing with us their views of presidential television: David Broder, reporter and political columnist, the *Washington Post;* Dean Burch, Chairman, Federal Communications Commission; Joseph Califano, attorney, formerly General Counsel to the Democratic National Committee; John Chancellor, reporter and commentator, NBC News; Murray Chotiner, attorney and political strategist, advisor to President Richard Nixon; Marcus Cohn, attorney; Jack Conway, President, Common Cause; Geoffrey Cowan, attorney; Frederick Dutton, author and political strategist, formerly assistant to President John F. Kennedy; Thomas Ervin, Executive Vice President, National Broadcasting Company; Charles D. Ferris, Director and General Counsel, Senate Democratic Policy Committee; Robert H. Fleming, assistant to Rep. Abraham Kazen, formerly Deputy Press Secretary to President Lyndon Johnson; Fred W. Friendly, Advisor to the President, Ford Foundation, Professor, Columbia University School of Journalism; Henry Geller, Special Assistant to the Chairman for Planning, Federal Communications Commission, formerly General Counsel, Federal Communications Commission; Mark Goode, Special Assistant to President Richard Nixon; Jack Gould, formerly television critic, the *New York Times;* James Haggerty, Vice President, American Broadcasting Company, formerly Press Secretary to President Dwight Eisenhower; John W. Hushen, Director of Public Information, U.S. Department of Justice; Richard Jencks, Vice President, Columbia Broadcasting System; Frank Jordan, Washington Bureau Chief, NBC News; Rod Keiser, Press Secretary to Rep. Carl Albert, Speaker of the House; Albert Kramer, Director, Citizens Communications Center; Laurence Laurent, television critic, the *Washington Post;* Peter Lisagor, Washington Bureau Chief, *Chicago Daily News;* John Lynch, Washington Bureau Chief, ABC News; Rep. Torbert H. Macdonald (D-Mass.), Chairman, Subcommittee on Communications and Power of the House Committee on Interstate and Foreign Commerce; Robert MacNeil, Senior

Correspondent, National Public Affairs Center for Television; Thomas Matthews, Vice President, Common Cause; Lyn Nofziger, Deputy Chairman, Republican National Committee; W. Theodore Pierson, Sr., attorney, Special Counsel to the Republican National Committee; Hoyt H. Purvis, Press Secretary to Sen. J. W. Fulbright; Benjamin Raub, Vice President and Assistant General Attorney, National Broadcasting Company; George Reedy, Woodrow Wilson International Center for Scholars, formerly Press Secretary to President Lyndon Johnson; Gerald Slater, General Manager, Public Broadcasting Service; William Small, Washington Bureau Chief, CBS News; Howard K. Smith, reporter and commentator, ABC News; John Stewart, Director, Office of Communications, Democratic National Committee; David J. Webster, Director of U.S. Operations, British Broadcasting Corporation; Gordon Weil, formerly Press Secretary to Sen. George McGovern; Tracy Weston, attorney, Stern Community Law Firm; Rep. Lester L. Wolff (D-N.Y.); Nicholas Zapple, Counsel, Senate Committee on Commerce; Ronald Ziegler, Press Secretary to President Richard Nixon.

NEWTON N. MINOW
JOHN BARTLOW MARTIN
LEE M. MITCHELL

PRESIDENTIAL TELEVISION

CHAPTER 1

POLITICS AND TELEVISION

ON THE EVENING of July 15, 1971, a spokesman for the Western White House at San Clemente, California told the three major television networks that President Richard M. Nixon had an announcement he wanted to make on nationwide television. The networks quickly cleared time for the announcement, which would interrupt their regular shows at 10:30: "The Dean Martin Show," a rerun of "NYPD," and a 1968 movie entitled *Counterfeit Killer*. But even after agreeing to the presidential preemption, the networks did not know the subject of the president's address. Network newsmen with the president in California received neither advance copies of his statement nor pre-broadcast briefings; they were as much in the dark as anyone else at air time. Promptly at 10:30 P.M., from NBC studios in Burbank, California, the president's image appeared in 25 million homes across the country. "I have requested this television time tonight," he said, "to announce a major development in our efforts to build a lasting peace in the world." He then told the American people he had accepted an invitation from Premier Chou En-lai to visit mainland China. At the same time, he revealed that his chief foreign policy adviser, Henry Kissinger, had secretly spent three days in China already.

President Nixon's dramatic announcement of a major reversal of U.S. foreign policy took the news media, the American public, and the rest of the world completely by surprise. And its impact was greatly increased because he made it directly and personally to the American people. One professional observer, calling this use of television a "bombshell approach to major new announcements," wrote that such an approach almost guaranteed that the first wave of news coverage would be extremely heavy and would be limited to straight reporting, thus giving the new policy powerful momentum—and momentum without critical appraisal: "Surprise makes for confusion and, at least initially, confusion does not make for valuable analysis." [1]

Time and again, and in recent years with increasing frequency, presidents have appeared on television to explain their policies, to mobilize support, to go over the heads of the Congress and the political parties, and to speak directly to the people for their cause—and their reelection.

Television has made it possible for a president to appear and speak directly before the entire American people. Not speeches on the stump, not speeches from the rear platforms of trains, not courthouse square handshaking, not newspapers, not magazines, not books, and not even radio can confront so many people with the president's face and with his words at the moment he utters them. Television, and only television, allows the president to exhibit his plans, opinions, and personality to the eyes and ears of unprecedented numbers of Americans—in their homes, but in his own way and under his control. As a result, television has become an increasingly important part of the complex power structure of presidential politics.

Television (complemented by radio) has come to play a significant role in presidential politics because it is the most effective communicator of ideas and images, with the greatest potential for influencing public opinion, that political man has yet developed. "Wherever one goes in America, there is radio and television," says a report of the Corporation for Public Broadcasting. "Fly over the heartland and see the antennas glinting. Ride an elevated through the ghetto of a large city on any evening and from thousands of darkened rooms witness the screen's glow. Zoom along a super highway, or bump along a back rural road, and zooming or bumping with you is radio. Unquestionably, one of the things all Americans have in common is radio and television." [2]

Hyperbole aside, it is estimated that 97 percent of the population possess at least one television receiver [3] and that the average set operates more than seven hours per day.[4] In 1972, there were more than nine hundred licensed television stations in the country, with some major cities being served by as many as ten television stations and a considerably greater number of radio stations. Commissioner Nicholas Johnson of the Federal Communications Commission estimates that "the average male viewer, between his second and sixty-fifth year, will watch television for over 3000 entire days—roughly, nine full years of his life. During the average weekday winter evening nearly half of the American people are to be found silently seated with fixed gaze upon a phosphorescent screen." [5] According to another expert, "by the time an American child is eighteen years old he has spent twenty thousand hours in front of his television set, more time than he has spent in classrooms, churches, and all other educational and cultural activities." [6]

A congressional subcommittee has found that "broadcasting, and television in particular, has indeed become indispensable to the political processes of our nation. This has come about because the medium—for whatever reason—has become the public's prime source of information." [7] One survey made in 1971 indicated that television is the primary source of news for most people; according to other surveys, people consider television the most objective and believable of all the mass media.[8]

Television's combination of ideas, moving pictures, and easy accessibility is unmatched by any other medium. Television and television alone has made the people eyewitnesses to history: the muffled drums and riderless horse at President Kennedy's funeral, Ruby shooting Oswald, the burning huts and crying children of Vietnam, the first man on the moon, triumph and tragedy at Munich's Olympics, the American president toasting the Communist chieftain in the Great Hall of the People in Peking. When Martin Luther King, Jr. was assassinated, television so shortened reaction time that within hours of the first televised civil disturbances, riots broke out in more than a hundred cities.[9]

Erik Barnouw has suggested that the nation's radio-television complex serves as a political nervous system: "It sorts and distributes information, igniting memories. . . . The impulses it transmits can stir the juices of emotion and can trigger action. As in the case of a central nervous system, aberrations can deeply disturb the body politic." [10]

But television's most significant political characteristic probably is its ability to present an image of a politician—providing an indication of his character and personality. An aspiring political leader today is likely to rise faster and further if he "comes across" well on television. Citizens in the television age expect their leaders to be reasonably pleasing to the eye and to be capable of a confidence-inspiring television presentation. "As a result of continual exposure to television," writes an experienced political television adviser, "we have learned to project characteristics of our television heroes to our political heroes. We want them to be articulate and also look competent. . . ." [11] Consequently, it is not unusual for politicians at all levels to hire television advisers, speech therapists, makeup art-ists, or other professionals to work on the leader's television image. The electoral success of such political figures as John and Robert Kennedy, Senators Percy and Tunney, Governor Reagan and Mayor Lindsay is often credited, at least in part, to their creation of a favorable television image.

If a good television image helps a politician, a poor one can hurt. Lyndon Johnson, for example, rarely appeared to good advantage on television despite a great deal of personal effort and professional advice. When he appeared before the large television audiences, his image, in the words of one critic, "stuck to the lens." But such is the power and prestige of the presidency that each of his television appearances exposed that image to millions. When Johnson finally announced on all three major television networks simultaneously that he would not run for reelection, he faced an audience of 75 million people. In comparison, when George Washington made the same announcement 172 years earlier, his words, without any image, took four days to reach New York in print and ten days to reach outlying regions.

Researchers still argue over whether television changes or merely reinforces opinions, but they generally agree that it can promote familiarity with an image or a personality, whether real or manufactured, with considerable success. In 1952, some of Adlai E. Stevenson's supporters felt that because he did not have a strong television presence he would have been better off had he come to presidential candidacy before televison. On the other hand, when he was nominated during the summer he was merely a little-known governor; by November, he was a national and even an international figure, thanks in large part to television.

Recognizing the pervasiveness of television, its role as the electorate's main source of political information, and its ability to convey images, candidates for election to public office have embraced the public airwaves with enthusiasm. By a television appearance, a politician may place his views before a potentially enormous audience; by appearing simultaneously on most major television channels, so that alternative viewing choices are sharply limited, he can assure that much of the potential will be realized. If a viewer is not sufficiently resistant to turn his set off, the political message generally gets through, as one analyst has noted:

> When asked, they say that they dislike political broadcasts . . . but when there is no alternative, they watch. There is good reason to believe, moreover, that these are people who were *not* previously reached. . . . Television has "activated" them: they have political opinions, and talk to others about them. It can be demonstrated that they have learned something—even when their viewing was due more to lack of alternatives than to choice.[12]

Television's role in elections has become so important that the *New York Times* assigned a reporter to cover the 1972 elections from in front of a television set. The paper was acknowledging that the way the candidates appear on television can be a critical factor in the election and that much of the candidates' other activities—the traveling, the dinner speeches, the factory and shopping-center visits—are done as much to gain television news exposure as for any other purpose.[13] Although social scientists and political experts have yet to determine the precise effect of television political advertising on the outcome of an election campaign, most candidates are not willing to take chances.[14] As any television viewer can attest, candidates do their best to saturate the airwaves with their messages.

But television advertising is expensive, and the candidates' rush to television has skyrocketed the cost of running for office. In the 1970 nonpresidential elections, candidates spent $58 million on political broadcasting, almost doubling the broadcast expenses of the previous off-year elections.[15] The three senatorial candidates in New York spent an incredible total of $5 million, more than $2 million of it on television and radio broadcasting.[16] Even running for such a modest office as congressman from the First District in Utah requires at least $70,000.[17] These enormous costs present a real danger to the political system. Robert Bendiner in the *New York Times* notes that "to get elected to high public office today, a candidate must either be a man in the top tax brackets himself or, more serious, a man unhealthily dependent on those who are and have axes to grind." [18] Certainly the high cost of campaign advertising can allow a heavily financed candidate to dominate the most important means of communication, adding credence to the cynics' view that politics is but a rich man's game. As a report by the Committee for Economic Development concluded, "any possibility of monopolistic manipulation or inequitable access" to political television because of its costs would "constitute the gravest kind of danger to our democratic political system." [19]

Growing public uneasiness about the money pressures on candidates has led to two recent legislative reforms. First, Congress adopted a law that will allow each citizen, by marking his annual tax return, to contribute one dollar to the party of his choice or to a general campaign fund to assist in financing the campaigns of major party candidates for the presidency.[20] Second, Congress enacted a requirement that broadcasters charge candidates only their very lowest rates for political broadcasting time. Congress also established a limit on the amount that could be spent by candidates for the purchase of broadcast time.[21] These two reforms are expected to reduce the danger of abuse.

But the power of political television is not limited to individual candidates or to election campaign periods. Senator Edmund Muskie has even testified that "used to its fullest, television can determine the outcome not only of every political issue, but more importantly of each and every national issue." [22] The success of candidates' use of television has given rise to presidential television—the use of television (and radio) by an already elected president to advance his legislative programs and his political objectives. The public and Congress have turned their attention to financial and fairness problems resulting from the use of television by candidates but have paid relatively little attention to the rampant growth of presidential television. Yet presidential television may damage democratic institutions even more than campaign television.

The Constitution established a presidency with limitations upon its powers—the need to stand for reelection every four years, checks that can be exercised by the Congress and the Supreme Court. The evolution of political parties and a strong two-party system provided a rallying point for opponents of an incumbent administration, enhancing the importance of frequent reelection. An intricate set of constitutional balances limiting the powers of each of the three government branches added force to the separation of government functions. These political and constitutional relationships served the country well for many years. Television's impact, however, threatens to tilt the delicately balanced system in the direction of the president.

By transmitting information and images effectively, television influences public opinion; public opinion is the key to the maintenance of political power. Plato reasoned that because a leader must seek public support if he is to govern effectively, the population of a city should be the number of people who can hear the leader's voice. Abraham Lincoln wrote that in politics, "public sentiment is everything. With public sentiment, nothing can fail. Without it nothing can succeed." [23] Professor Richard Neustadt, whose model of a powerful presidency was sought by President Kennedy, observed that "presidential power is the power to persuade." [24] Because he can act while his adversaries can only talk, because he can make news and draw attention to himself, and because he is the only leader elected by all the people, an incumbent president always has had an edge over his opposition in persuading public opinion. Presidential television, however, has enormously increased that edge.

Presidential television means the ability to appear simultaneously on all national radio and television networks at prime, large-audience evening hours, virtually whenever and however the president wishes. It means holding a news conference before a potential audience of 60 million people, or delivering light banter on the country's most popular entertainment programs. Presidential television is the president's own explanation of his plans and positions to politicians, legislators, and voters —the national audience of millions. It is the carefully presented presidential "image." It is the nationally viewed justification of war, invocation of peace, praise for political allies, damnation of opponents, veto of legislation, scolding of Congress by a chief executive, commander-in-chief, party leader, and candidate.

Presidential television is free use of an extremely expensive commodity. An individual or group wishing to broadcast a half-hour program simultaneously on all three major networks during evening prime time could pay more than $250,000, exclusive of the cost of producing the program, assuming that the time could be bought—which in all probability it could not. But a president, as Senator Fulbright has noted, can "command a national audience to hear his views on controversial matters at prime time, on short notice, at whatever length he chooses, and at no expense to the Federal Government or his party." [25] Or himself.

The continued ability of the opposition political party to pose a realistic election threat, the continued ability of Congress to withstand presidential pressure, and even the continued ability of the Supreme Court to maintain its independence from political pressures, depend on keeping the balance between them and the president. Given the president's special access to television, it may be necessary to give these institutions sufficient access of their own to the public through television. Reviewing President Truman's seizure of the steel mills in 1952, the Supreme Court noted that through public opinion the president "exerts a leverage upon those who are supposed to check and balance his power which often cancels their effectiveness." [26] Public opinion has historically enabled opposition parties, the Supreme Court, and the Congress to act as a rein on the executive and preserve the two-party political system. "Public opinion," Clinton Rossiter has noted, helps to check presidential power "when it encourages Congress to override a veto, persuades an investigating committee to put a White House intimate on the grill, stiffens the resolve of a band of Senators to talk until Christmas . . . and puts backbone in a Supreme Court asked to nullify a Presidential order. The various institutions and centers of power that check the President are inept and often useless without public opinion." [27] If the president's naturally preeminent position becomes a virtual monopoly of political communication, presidential television can constitute a danger to democracy.

Other countries have experienced similar television monopolies under circumstances that can only be considered ominous. Adolf Hitler, who employed his monopoly over German radio with great effectiveness, was intrigued by television's manipulative potential; his scientists, before being diverted by wartime urgencies, developed a closed-circuit system that Hitler once used to broadcast an announcement to an audience watching his image on a large theater screen. Fidel Castro spent hours under klieg lights during the months in which he consolidated his victory in the Cuban revolution. Gamal Abdel Nasser, too, built a television system in Egypt to advance his political fortunes. His technicians even developed battery-powered television for use in villages lacking electricity. Nasser's broadcasting was filled with subtle propaganda, but because he was afraid of overexposure, Nasser himself rarely appeared on television.[28]

Unlike Hitler's Germany or Castro's Cuba or Nasser's United Arab Republic, the problem in this country is not that of a total monopoly. The Congress and the opposition party are not completely barred from television. Far from it. Network interview programs regularly feature political and congressional leaders, and it is a rare newscast that does not offer a glimpse of a party or congressional figure voicing opposition to the president's viewpoint. Traditionally, responses to a presidential State of the Union address are broadcast by one or more of the major networks. The networks also produce "specials" from time to time that have presented reactions to presidential policy statements. Nevertheless, newscasts and specials are not the same form of access that the president enjoys. In appearances on presidential television, he controls the programs; the opposition does not. Richard S. Salant, president of CBS News, acknowledges that while the president's political and congressional opposition is frequently heard on news and documentary programs, these broadcasts generally are internally balanced and, unlike presidential television, not intended to persuade. "Further, the participants in these . . . broadcasts do not have the advantages which the president has—the live, unedited appearance, the direct presentation free of journalists' questioning, the simultaneous appearance on all networks, and the control of timing and place in the broadcast schedule." [29]

Congressmen supporting a move to override a presidential veto of legislation—a veto message delivered by a president before millions of television viewers—are not likely to be able to command free, prime, simultaneous three-network broadcast time for their side of the issue to quell the flow of constituent mail generated by the president's appearance; the leading opposition party figure is not likely to be able to command free, prime, simultaneous three-network broadcast time to state his position on an issue discussed by the president in an appearance just ninety days before a presidential election. As one interested group sees it, it is "as if the President has a megaphone and a soapbox while everyone else is required to whisper." [30]

Many believe too, that television has contributed to the weakening of the political parties in the last decades. Before television, a candidate depended upon the party organization, especially on the precinct captains, to take his cases to the voters. But today the candidate can speak directly to the voters in their homes. As a result, the party label has become less important than the man who wears it.

Of late, numerous small special-interest organizations such as Common Cause have demanded television time to raise new issues for national debate or to respond to issues set forth in presidential television appearances. Each group wants to present its views not through interviews, panels, commentators, newsmen or network-produced specials, but rather in broadcast time that, like the president's time, is under its own control. "In many places they are called coalitions," says *Broadcasting,* the leading industry news journal. "In some cities they are, simply, committees. But the aims of the members are the same: to gain access to the broadcasting media, to help set the agenda for American broadcasting." [31] They feel the issues are too important, too immediate, to leave to a broadcast licensee acting as "gatekeeper" to the airwaves. They want direct access to television on their own terms. "Broadcasting is so pervasive it has become a personal thing to them; they would feel they had a claim on it even if they had never heard that the airwaves belong to the public. And they all *have* heard that." [32]

A network executive has described the extent of the requests for access:

> Recent demands and requests included those received from the South Africa Foundation requesting time to refute alleged errors of fact in a CBS News documentary entitled "A Black View of South Africa" (the Foundation sought to have our

broadcast license renewals held up in the bargain); from the Credit Bureau of Greater Shreveport requesting time to respond to an interview which allegedly maligned the credit bureau industry; from Reverend Carl McIntire on behalf of United States March for Victory; from Lawrence F. O'Brien on behalf of the Democratic National Committee; from Common Cause asking to purchase time to present an antiwar documentary; from Governor Nunn of Kentucky requesting time to refute alleged news distortions concerning the tobacco industry; from Congressman Hogan requesting time to respond to Congressman Boggs' charges against the FBI; from Action for Alcoholism requesting time to present viewpoints contrary to those of alcoholic beverage advertisers; from the Communications Workers of America requesting the purchase of a half hour to discuss the state of negotiations between the union and the telephone company; and from Congressman William L. Clay on behalf of the Black Caucus.

These individuals and groups were but a small vanguard of an army of partisans prepared to seek direct access to the air. Some others were already on the sidelines. An organization called Tell It to Hanoi Committee warned us that if Common Cause were given time, they also would need it. Doubtless if the Communications Workers had been permitted to tell their story directly, the Bell System would have wanted to do likewise. And if the Black Caucus, or any other racial or ethnic group within the Congress, had obtained time to respond to the president's State of the Union message, there is every reason to believe that other racial and ethnic groups of Congressmen would seek similar time.[33]

Speaking to a group of broadcasters in 1971, the chairman of the Federal Communications Commission remarked that "in a real sense, your industry is the victim of its own success. It's a vital medium. The public wants in. And a growing crowd of individuals and groups are *demanding* access." [34] The number and vociferousness of these demands suggest that the public institutions designed to counterbalance the presidential appeal to the power of public opinion are not adequately performing their function. The fault does not appear to be theirs so much as it is the growing power of the presidency, aided by presidential television.

Little less than fifty years ago, virtually all government interest in broadcasting occupied but a small part of the time of a House of Representatives' Committee on Merchant Marine and Fisheries; radio was primarily used for ship-to-shore communication. Nevertheless, that committee dimly glimpsed broadcasting's future and, in an early report, listed among the "possibilities and potentialities" of the medium a substantial "political" role.[35] By the 1970s it was acknowledged that broadcasting, and particularly television, had become a powerful political weapon in reaching elective office and in governing once there. The chairman of the Senate Communications Subcommittee, which devotes almost all its attention to broadcasting, observes that a political candidate easily can reach more than 20 million voters—one-third of the number that voted in the 1968 presidential election—with one appearance on one television network for just one minute.[36] And once in office that candidate can use television to sell his program, his party, and himself.

CHAPTER 2

THE BULLY PULPIT

THE PRESIDENT HAS a wide choice of radio and television techniques. He may make a formal address, hold a press conference, consent to an interview, telephone an astronaut, go to a football game, receive a visiting chief of state, take a trip abroad, or play with his dog on the White House lawn. He may send his family, his cabinet members, or his political allies before the cameras. In almost every case, he, and he alone, decides. His ability to choose when and how to appear without cost before millions of viewers is completely unmatched by his political or Congressional opponents.

The most direct form of presidential television is the formal address preempting regular television programs to announce an important event or policy decision. For some years, whenever a president has wished to address the nation, a White House aide simply has relayed the request to the Washington bureau chief of one of the three major networks. The bureau chief, designated coordinator on a rotating basis by his colleagues at the other two networks, quickly informs them of the request. A presidential request for television time has never been rejected. If the White House aide has requested a particular time in the broadcast day, the networks usually have cleared that time for the president, even when it has required considerable juggling of the evening's entertainment schedule. Occasionally the networks have suggested a different time from the one requested; negotiation has proved easy. The three networks usually carry the president's message simultaneously, with the result that in cities served only by network-affiliated stations, viewers have no choice of what to watch; in larger cities, viewing choices are diminished. Presidential television addresses usually are carried at the same time by all major radio networks. More and more, the televised presidential address has been delivered during prime time, the 7:00–11:00 P.M. period during which commercial broadcasting attracts the largest audience.

The formal presidential television address or announcement is a powerful instrument. With as much or as little time as he chooses, with control over format and visual techniques, with the built-in audience for prime-time entertainment, and unimpeded by questions, the president can carefully develop and argue for a policy decision. He can thus present a complex or controversial position effectively, perhaps uniting a divided citizenry on an international issue, creating public support for a legislative initiative, or simply avoiding the necessity of having his views questioned by a skeptical press.

A presidential address carried simultaneously by the three major television networks can reach an audience of vast proportions. With more than 90 million television sets in the country, special television events, such as the first moon landing, have attracted over 100 million viewers. It is not unusual today for a prime-time presidential address to reach an audience of 70 million or more Americans. To reach an audience of that size in person, a president would have to appear before capacity crowds forty-eight times in each of the twenty-six mammoth stadiums used by professional football teams from Boston to San Diego—a total of 1,248 separate appearances.

Evidence indicates that the televised presidential address can have an important effect on public opinion of national issues. Polls have disclosed, for example, that public support for a Kennedy tax proposal rose by 4 percent after his television address on the subject; that support for President Johnson's position on Vietnam issues rose by 30 percent after one of his television addresses; and that support for President Nixon's Vietnam policies rose by 18 percent after one of his television addresses.[1] Louis Harris reports a definite "correlation between televised presidential speeches and increased public acceptance of the president's positions.[2]

Both Congress and the opposition political party have felt the sting of presidential attack or the pressure of presidential legislative proposal or veto delivered in a broadcast address. The presidency is inescapably political. As Tom Wicker of the *New York Times* observes, "almost no Presidential appearance of any consequence can be divorced entirely from its political impact." [3] Each television address by the president has the goal of convincing the public that the policies of the incumbent administration are superior to all others, including those advocated by the opposition party. The televised address determines which issues will appear on the national agenda—issues chosen by the president, not the opposition. Television, the opposition party once charged, "is at the call of the President . . . to lay the groundwork for his reelection in hour after hour of prime time." [4] Effectively used, the presidential television address can undermine the ability of the party out of power to mount an effective electoral challenge.

Through a televised address, the president can initiate popular legislation. If the legislation dies, the public, unaware of the complexities involved, will blame congressional inertia. Again, the president may use a televised address to nip in the bud a congressional uprising. Again, he may go on television to veto a bill and thus win popular support to sustain his veto. Congressmen report that presidential addresses often elicit a major flow of mail supporting the presidential position and even parroting his words. Several congressmen have observed that "network television has become a prime instrument of presidential power" while, "concurrently, the communications power of Congress has begun to wane." [5]

To reinforce his televised policy address and enhance his public image, the president may seek less formal TV appearances to create an image worthy of public trust, confidence, and support—news conferences, interviews, guest appearances on scheduled television programs, participation in events covered by TV, and activities that make news for the evening network news programs. These can be as effective as the formal address.

In these situations, the president surrenders some control over his presentation and may share the screen with others. This makes the presentation of detailed issues difficult. On the other hand, his audience may be larger than his audience for an address—an appearance at a major sports event, for example —and the president may be able to turn reporters' or interviewers' questions to his advantage. On informal television interview shows, the president may remind viewers that he is a family man, or a sports enthusiast, or a raconteur, or a sincere and likable person, a "regular guy." Candidates for public office work hard to convey such personality traits to voters. A president has more opportunity to do it than anyone else, not only during campaigns but throughout the four years between elections.

The least direct method of presidential television does not exhibit the president but rather consists of a wide variety of television appearances by members of his family, cabinet officers, or political allies. This may include televised tours of the White House led by the First Lady, a "Today" show interview with a top presidential adviser, even a White House wedding. Each department of the executive branch assigns personnel and spends money to provide national public information, including television programs. In 1971, the Interior Department hired a political television expert to make suggestions for improving the department's public relations; he recommended, among other things, that the department take advantage of "the rugged good looks" and the "star" quality of the Secretary of the Interior and put him on television more often.

Almost anything the president does is news. By virtue of his office, the president of the United States—its constitutional leader, supreme military commander, chief diplomat and administrator, and preeminent social host—obviously ranks higher in the scale of newsworthiness than anyone else—defeated opposition candidate, national party chairman, governor, congressman, senator. Time on the evening news programs is severely limited. But the president will have no difficulty getting on if he wants to. He alone can become news merely by going to church or walking in the White House garden.

A presidential press conference is clearly news. So is his televised address; a report of it will be on page 1 in tomorrow's newspapers. A presidential speech broadcast only on radio will be reported in the television news. Calvin Coolidge, campaigning for reelection in 1924, chose to avoid political meetings and to appear chiefly at dedications, historical anniversaries, meetings of commercial or religious groups. Even these appearances made news, simply because he was the president. When he chose election eve to address the Chamber of Commerce, his speech was broadcast coast to coast by twenty-three radio stations and "all other U.S. radio stations hushed their voices for forty-five minutes." [6]

The opposition can never equal the president's ability to make news. When, in the campaign of 1972, George McGovern, Democratic candidate for president, requested television time to explain why he had asked Senator Tom Eagleton to resign as his vice-presidential candidate, the networks refused on the grounds that his appearance would not be news unless he were to name Eagleton's successor—something he was not then prepared to do. It is hard to believe the networks would not have given President Nixon television time had he decided to drop Vice President Agnew from his ticket and asked for time to explain why. This is not for a minute to suggest that the networks are biased against the Democrats. It is merely to suggest the newsworthiness of the president of the United States.

Because of who he is, newsmen and their editors allow the president to speak for himself. The remarks of an opposition spokesman may be summarized in television news reporting or analysis; the president's views usually are given in his own words. If a president asks for time, network executives can hardly decide that what he wishes to say is less important than what Marcus Welby has to say. Moreover, they are hard put to determine what part of his discourse is most important, especially if he insists that it is all important.

Not only are broadcasters hesitant to edit or act as gatekeeper of the airwaves when the president is involved; they are equally hesitant to treat him roughly on the air. The president's preeminent position forbids harsh questions during televised press conferences or interviews. Although heads of government in such other countries as Great Britain are judged in part by how they handle public challenges to their policies, Americans do not like to see their president publicly challenged or embarrassed by hard questions. A newsman who presses the president too hard knows that he probably will not be allowed to do it again and that, moreover, his sources in the administration are likely to dry up. As Howard K. Smith, a veteran of several presidential interviews, has said, "The Chief of State is like the flag. You have to be deferential." [7]

Television today means networks. Of the approximately 700 licensed commercial TV stations, more than 80 percent are affiliated with one of the three major television networks. The network provides programs for local affiliates. It sells spot advertising time for broadcast during the programs and splits the income with the stations. Sometimes it allows the affiliates to sell spots themselves. Network-originated programming consumes three quarters of the big-audience, prime-time viewing hours as well as significant daytime periods. What the networks choose to carry, and what they believe will be profitable to carry, is what the vast majority of viewers will see.

"To the critic, television is about programs," says *Variety* writer Les Brown, but "to the broadcast practitioner, it is mainly about sales." [8] Broadcasting is a business, with profit and loss statements, stockholders, and a rewards system that favors fiscal excellence above information excellence. Because of the vital importance of audience size, the networks spend much time and energy devising schedules that will attract and retain large numbers of viewers each day. Programs come and go and schedules are juggled endlessly to maximize the network's share of the total television audience. FCC Commissioner Nicholas Johnson, a leading critic of commercial broadcasting, has created a parable describing how a group of citizens went to the broadcast industry to ask for, or even to pay for, time to present informative programming on the issues of the day, only to be told by the broadcasters that "there was no longer any room at their inn for the discussion of public issues—like war, and life, and politics—because the time all had to be used for programs and announcements necessary to the very difficult but essential task of manipulating consumers to buy useless and harmful products." [9]

Unlike Commissioner Johnson's mythical group, however, a president that goes on television will not necessarily doom the network to a small audience. Although his audience appeal may be far less than that of a Dean Martin or Lucille Ball, a highly touted presidential television appearance does have the potential to attract large audiences; the public feels the president may say something "new" and important, and often he does. Because of the general interest in presidential activities, broadcasters believe a TV "special" on a president's trip or on the Christmas plans of the White House family are programs that can attract a reasonable audience. Even if a presidential appearance produces a low audience, it is not a total loss to the networks; the president has given them prestige, and networks feel that prestige in turn can attract more viewers to their regular programs. In part for this reason, if one network decides to carry a presidential appearance, the others will do so too, for fear of missing out on a prestigious occasion.

A president is further assured of broadcast time because broadcasters are eager to please him. They are, after all, licensed by the federal government, by the Federal Communications Commission. And the president appoints the members of the FCC. Broadcasting is not a right; it is a privilege, revocable by the FCC. Since television stations are enormously valuable, commonly worth many millions of dollars, broadcast executives admit to being sensitive about incurring the displeasure of the president and his FCC. A former network correspondent, Robert MacNeil, has written that broadcasters view their relationship with the president "through the eyes of the businessman [and] see immense power which—if crossed—might harm

[them]." [10] Network men acknowledge they are "prone, perhaps unconsciously, to think twice and perhaps decide on the side of caution" in decisions involving any possibility of government regulatory retaliation.[11]

Occupants of the White House have not hesitated to capitalize on broadcaster fears of retaliation. Franklin Roosevelt let the industry know that FCC policies could begin at the White House. President Johnson was quick to let broadcasters know in no uncertain terms when they displeased him. Vice President Agnew has charged broadcasters with being unfair to the president, while reminding them that they operate under government licenses.[12] Whether intentional or not, the incumbent exercises power over broadcast decision-making. A study by the *Columbia Journal of Law and Social Problems* labeled this the "subtlest aspect" of presidential dominance of television.[13]

The only restriction upon a president's use of television is imposed not by the broadcasters but by the audience. Franklin Roosevelt once observed that "the public psychology . . . cannot, because of human weakness, be attuned for long periods of time to a constant repetition of the highest note in the scale." [14] At some point too much presidential television exposure will bore the public.

Over the years, successive presidents have recognized their inherent media advantages. Presidential manipulation of the media began long before television. In the early days of the republic, presidents used newspapers to persuade the public of the wisdom of their leadership. George Washington, considering a draft of an important presidential message, is said to have worried that it might be too long for newspaper publication. Andrew Jackson confounded his critics by adding fifty-seven journalists to the government payroll, inspiring charges of "rule by newspaper." [15] Calvin Coolidge, too, was accused of using newspapers for "propaganda purposes." [16]

Before radio or television, Theodore Roosevelt termed the office of the presidency a "bully pulpit" because of the opportunity it gave him to preach his gospel to the American people. Broadcasting added powerful new communications capabilities to a president's "bully pulpit." For the first time, the president could reach, instantaneously and simultaneously, a majority of the people in the country, not through a journalist's account, but in his own words and voice. Far more than print, broadcasting is intimately connected with presidential politics. By definition, presidential politics is national; only broadcasting blankets the whole nation instantly. As time passed, presidents increasingly went on the air not only to advocate legislation and explain peril but also to enhance their personal images in the voters' minds.

One of the first radio broadcasts to the public was a postelection report on the 1916 Wilson-Hughes campaign delivered on an experimental station in New York State. The beginning of modern commercial radio is often traced to the broadcast of election results by station KDKA in Pittsburgh in 1920. It was this election reporting that first brought radio's potential to the attention of politicians.

Woodrow Wilson had observed that "one of the serious difficulties of politics in the country . . . is provincialism— the general absence of national information and national opinion." [17] As a consequence, he took his argument for the League of Nations to the country overland, traveling eight thousand miles, delivering thirty-seven separate speeches and ruining his health—all in vain. Wilson was the first president to deliver a speech on radio, but because of poor reception, listeners could distinguish only a few random words.

When Warren Harding ascended to the presidency in 1921, radio was still more a curiosity than a political tool. After venturing onto the airways for the first time, he received telegrams reporting "we heard you as plainly as if you had been in our living room" and completely ignoring the content of his broadcast.[18] But by 1923, Harding had made a number of live radio addresses explaining and defending his administration. Harding was the first president who used radio to explain executive decisions. In June 1923, his speech on the World Court was carried by a "presidential network" of radio stations specially created for that purpose.

But in his pursuit of public support for his World Court policy, Harding still found it necessary to travel the country. His railroad car was equipped with a radio transmitter so his speeches could be broadcast as he traveled, but he had difficulty adjusting to radio. The *New York Times* observed that Harding was "dominated by the restraining influence of the radio-telephone amplifiers. . . . The mechanical contrivance worries him . . . and he is tempted at times to revert to the old style of direct oratory, more stimulating to both orator and audience." [19] When Vice President Calvin Coolidge took office after Harding's death, the budding radio industry called on him to conserve his health by using radio's capability to communicate with the country.[20]

Coolidge's 1924 campaign gave rise to the first charges of unequal radio treatment of the candidates. Coolidge's inaugural address, following that campaign, was carried live by twenty-one radio stations to approximately 15 million people.[21] Although Coolidge was called Silent Cal, in his first year in office, he spoke an average of nine thousand words per month into radio microphones (usually on noncontroversial subjects). His speeches reached more people than ever before in history— an estimated 50 million in one eight-month period alone.[22] Once in 1924 President Coolidge and an enterprising radio announcer stood together on a railroad platform in Glendale, California, with the following results:

> At once the radio announcer throbbed into the mike: "And *now*, ladies and gentlemen, for a real, new 'first' in history, you

will hear the *voice* of the President of the United States *over the radio!* . . . Mr. President, may I ask you to tell this audience, on a nationwide hookup, just as you are about to board this train back to Washington after a prolonged trip around the country: What message do you have for the American people?"

He tilted the microphone toward the pursed lips of President Coolidge, who opened them long enough to say: "Goodbye."

They don't make Presidents like that anymore.[23]

Herbert Hoover, Coolidge's Secretary of Commerce, led the successful campaign for passage of the Federal Radio Act of 1927, the first comprehensive governmental regulation of broadcasting. Hoover recognized that "radio has become a social force of the first order . . . revolutionizing the political debates that underlie political action [and making] us literally one people upon all occasions of general public interest." [24] As president, he spoke on radio many times but made no real effort to exploit the medium's political potential. Rejecting a suggestion that he make a live radio speech every week, Hoover said, "It is very difficult to deal with anything over the radio except generalities, without embarrassing actual accomplishments which are going forward." [25] As a result, the best-remembered Hoover radio speech is known not for its content but for the introduction given by announcer Harry Von Zell: "Ladies and gentlemen, the President of the United States, Hoobert Heever."

Franklin D. Roosevelt, Hoover's successor in the White House, was the first president to take full advantage of broadcasting. By the time he took office, radio had come of age technologically, and governmental regulation had made headway against interference among stations. The newspapers, largely Republican-owned, had been hostile to Roosevelt while he was governor of New York and remained hostile when he became president. Both as governor and president, Roosevelt used radio to bypass the press and take his case directly to the people. Roosevelt declared that broadcasting was "one of the most effective mediums for dissemination of information. It cannot misrepresent or misquote." [26] As one present-day observer notes, "Roosevelt showed the way and the Presidents have been off to the races ever since." [27]

Roosevelt began the practice of requesting time from the radio networks for live simultaneous nationwide broadcast. In addition, to protect his access to the people, he considered driving newspaper publishers from the broadcasting business. Shortly after election to his third term, finding that more than a third of all radio stations were owned or controlled by newspapers, Roosevelt sent a one-sentence memo to FCC Chairman James Lawrence Fly: "Will you let me know when you propose to have a hearing on newspaper ownership of radio stations?" [28] Fly was willing to look into the question but was deeply involved in other matters and never held the hearing. At one point, President Roosevelt quietly explored the possibility of a government "clear channel" network, ostensibly as an information service to broadcast agricultural and weather reports, for example, but also, presumably, to be available for political speeches as well. The project was dropped, however, because the radio spectrum at that time was fully occupied.[29]

The first of Roosevelt's famous "fireside chats" was delivered at the end of his first week in office to a stricken nation—to a frightened people, to men in breadlines, to families losing their homes or savings. FDR's strong, yet soothing, voice healed the nation's spirit (and saved its banks). Will Rogers wrote, "America hasn't been so happy in three years as they are today, no banks, no work, no nothing. . . . They know they got a man in there who is wise to Congress, wise to our so-called big men. The whole country is with him, just so he does something." [30]

People who lived through those years retain the impression that FDR was almost constantly speaking to them in his fireside chats; in fact, he delivered only four during his first four years in office, four in his second term, and twelve in his third term. They averaged half an hour each. Almost all were delivered during the largest audience hours of 9:00 to 11:00 P.M., EST.[31] One listener marveled at Roosevelt's "ability to create a feeling of intimacy between himself and his listeners, his skill in placing emphasis on key words, his adroitness in presenting complicated matters in such simple terms that the man in the street believes he has a full mastery of them." [32] John Dos Passos described Roosevelt's as "the patroon voice, the headmaster's admonishing voice, the bedside doctor's voice that spoke to each man and to all of us." [33] FDR understood that radio was not just an adjunct to a podium but a new and different political medium.

The Roosevelt fireside chats reached audiences of unprecedented size, as the public came to depend on broadcasting for word of major political events. Roosevelt's first fireside chat was estimated to have reached 64 percent of all radio receivers, among the largest audiences in radio broadcast history.[34] By 1941, the radio audiences for FDR's speeches averaged an estimated 60 million people. Almost 80 percent of the homes in America heard the president's address following Pearl Harbor as he asked Congress for a declaration of war.[35]

In one of his fireside chats, Roosevelt urged listeners to write to him. "Tell me your troubles," he said, and soon he began receiving thousands of letters daily. For years, even through World War I and the stock market crash, one employee had handled presidential mail; but in March 1933, in response to FDR broadcasts, a backlog of half a million letters piled up.[36] Congress, too, was often swamped with mail after a Roosevelt radio address.

In addition to his fireside chats, FDR made hundreds of traditional live radio speeches, becoming so accustomed to the microphone that he once joked that he would have to become a radio commentator when he retired.[37] During his first ten months in office, Roosevelt delivered at least twenty live radio addresses.[38] His speeches united the country.

Roosevelt made unprecedented use of radio to mobilize popular support of his legislative proposals.[39] Radio helped the country to understand the New Deal program of social and economic legislation, and to overcome Congress's reluctance to give the federal government responsibilities it had never before undertaken.[40] Roosevelt himself acknowledged the part that radio had played in his success:

> Time after time, in meeting legislative opposition . . . , I have taken an issue directly to the voter by radio, and invariably I have met a most heartening response. Amid many developments of civilization which lead away from direct government by the people, the radio is one which tends on the other hand to restore direct contact between the masses and their chosen leaders.[41]

At the end of Roosevelt's first hundred days in office, "he had only to glance toward a microphone or suggest that he might go on the air again and a Congressional delegation would surrender." [42] The *New York Times* observed that FDR's "use of this new instrument of political discussion is a plain hint to Congress of a recourse which the President may employ if it proves necessary to rally support for legislation which he asks and which the lawmakers might be reluctant to give him." Roosevelt was utterly unabashed about what he was doing. Seeking to prevent Congress from overriding his veto of a bill he considered inflationary, he announced the veto in a radio broadcast: "I'm going to put it right to the housewife. Maybe she can hold the boys in line better than I can." [43]

FDR set the precedent for evening broadcast of the president's annual State of the Union message to Congress. In 1936, over strenuous Republican protests, Roosevelt succeeded in arranging for Congress to hold an unusual joint session at 9:00

P.M. instead of the traditional noon hour, so that his State of the Union address could be broadcast live to the large evening radio audience.[44] In 1944, Roosevelt was ill and sent his State of the Union speech to the Capitol by messenger—but nine hours later, from the White House, he broadcast the speech to home listeners.

Presidential broadcasts provoked virtually no controversy when their purpose was clearly to inform the public, and relatively little when they were designed to put pressure on Congress. But during the 1936 and 1940 campaigns, Roosevelt caused a furor by asking for and receiving free radio time as president to make what his opponents considered electioneering speeches. Two Los Angeles radio stations refused to broadcast his 1936 fireside chats. The stations' general manager announced that Roosevelt's remarks would be broadcast free "when he is officiating as President rather than a candidate for office. . . . But if he seeks to use the facilities of KFI or KECA in the interest of reelection, we must necessarily answer negatively any request or demand for free time." [45] The controversy over free presidential radio time increased in 1940 when the National Association of Broadcasters suggested that other candidates should bear the burden of proving a Roosevelt address "political" before a station refused the president free time.[46]

FDR was the first president who utilized those closely associated with him as radio spokesmen for his administration policies and decisions. During his first ten months in office, while he himself made 20 radio broadcasts, members of his cabinet made 107 and Eleanor Roosevelt made 17.[47]

Roosevelt was the first president to appear live on television; he formally opened an RCA experimental television exhibit at the New York World's Fair on April 30, 1939. But it was President Harry Truman who, eight years later, initiated presidential television.

In the first telecast made from the White House, President Truman launched the Food Conservation Program. Thereafter, television carried all the president's major addresses. Truman was the first president who hired a media adviser to coach his broadcast delivery and handle preparations. The adviser, Leonard Reinsch (who subsequently advised President Kennedy), tried in vain to change Truman's flat Missouri accent and rapid delivery. Truman once explained that he spoke so fast because he wanted to get a long, uninteresting radio speech over with. He might have made it shorter, but "a lot of nice people worked on the speech, and I didn't want to hurt their feelings." [48] Truman at times appeared oblivious to radio and television. He is said to have rarely listened to radio or watched television, and he was criticized for not using them to announce such important policy decisions as the decision to develop the hydrogen bomb. [49] But his television appearance in the summer of 1950, to announce the outbreak of the Korean War, was a landmark in the history of presidential television. Jack Gould of the *New York Times* wrote: "For the first time in a period of national emergency, the person at home not only heard the fateful call for sacrifices to preserve his freedom, but also saw the grave expressions of the President as he explained to the country what it would mean." [50] Truman used broadcasting in other times of national crisis—a railroad strike, a steel strike, a meat shortage. In 1946, when labor leader John L. Lewis announced he would take the coal miners out on strike, President Truman responded by declaring that he would appeal to the miners on nationwide radio to disregard the strike call. Shortly before Truman's scheduled speech, Lewis backed down and called off the strike. In 1951, when Truman was unable to settle a stalemated contract negotiation between the United Steelworkers and the major steel producers, he went on nationwide television to announce his seizure of the steel industry. The boldness of the announcement may have helped to make possible the execution of this extraordinary presidential order.[51]

Truman introduced several new techniques into presidential television. In 1950, he presided over the cabinet's first appearance on television—a CBS broadcast of a regular cabinet session. He also brought the presidential press conference part way into the electronic age; in 1951, for the first time, he allowed newsmen to tape the conferences so that they could check their notes. A little later, he allowed small portions of the recordings to be broadcast on radio.

By 1952, television had an audience large enough to claim attention in plans for the presidential campaign. Only a few people had owned television receivers in 1948, but by 1952 advertisers estimated there were 19 million television sets and some 58 million viewers in the country.[52] The networks carried the two party conventions live—the Taft-Eisenhower struggle and the Stevenson draft, both filled with high drama. Eisenhower and Stevenson waged the first television campaign in American history. And soon after Eisenhower took office, his press secretary, James Hagerty, announced: "We are in a day of a new medium—television. I would like to work out with television representatives . . . a system whereby the President could give talks to the people of the country—possibly press conferences—on television . . . about once a month." [53]

It did not happen immediately, however. The first television news conference was filmed on January 19, 1955, midway through Eisenhower's first term. None of Eisenhower's conferences was broadcast live, because of White House concern that the president might make a serious slip of the tongue, as indeed he did at his first news conference; in discussing Indochina, he inadvertently said that the situation in "Indonesia" was deteriorating rapidly. The White House allowed news conferences to be filmed but did not release the films until they had been checked by the president's press secretary, who retained the right to edit them.

When Eisenhower began admitting television cameras and sound equipment to his press conferences, the networks gladly made air time available at the pleasure of the president, and they have continued to do so ever since. Today John Lynch, ABC's Washington news bureau chief, calls it "a matter of course" that news conferences receive live simultaneous coverage by the three networks if permitted.[54]

During the Eisenhower years, the three major television networks formed an *ad hoc* committee to deal with the president's desire to deliver live addresses on television. If the president wanted a speech broadcast nationally, press secretary Hagerty would ask the committee for a specified period of time. Although the committee might suggest a somewhat different time period, it usually honored the administration's request for nationwide television time. But on at least one occasion, President Eisenhower's address on Quemoy and Matsu, the networks delayed a president's speech until after the end of prime time. And in 1961, when President Kennedy asked for a half hour of network time at 8:00 P.M. for an address intended to forestall violence at the University of Mississippi, the networks resisted and Kennedy settled for 10:00 P.M.—by which time rioting had already begun.[55] Not until President Johnson's term did the networks begin giving the president virtually any time slot he asked for.

When President Eisenhower (or his advisers) did not actively seek television coverage of an impending presidential speech, the White House simply notified the networks in advance so that they could cover it if they wished. They usually wished. Jack Gould observed that the Eisenhower administration could "turn television on or off as it deems expedient," and that Hagerty thus held "potentially a most awesome power." [56]

Like President Truman, President Eisenhower employed broadcasting in time of crisis—the Middle East crisis (October 1956), the Near East crisis (February 1957), the dispatch of federal troops to racially troubled Little Rock, Arkansas (September 1957), and the Berlin crisis (March 1959).[57]

Two crises coincided with the Eisenhower reelection campaign. After his heart attack in September 1955, he appeared on television and found that his appearance helped to reassure the nation that he could continue in office. Early in the reelection year of 1956 he gave a televised press conference, not so much to answer questions as to show the country he looked fit. The telecast was received in almost 12 million homes, an impressive figure for those days.[58] A few months later, Eisenhower underwent abdominal surgery; shortly thereafter, another televised news conference gave reassuring evidence of his fitness. The same year, only a few days before the presidential election, Eisenhower made a radio and television report to the nation on events in the Middle East. Although he emphasized that he was speaking not as a candidate but as president, the Democrats demanded and finally were given time for their candidate, Adlai Stevenson, to respond.

Truman had introduced television cameras to a cabinet meeting in 1950. In June 1953, Eisenhower produced, with the assistance of the Batten, Barton, Durstine, and Osborn advertising agency, a televised roundtable discussion among Secretary of the Treasury George M. Humphrey, Secretary of Agriculture Ezra Taft Benson, Attorney General Herbert Brownell, Secretary of Health, Education, and Welfare Oveta Culp Hobby, and himself. The program was carefully rehearsed in an effort to give an impression of spontaneity. The next year, Eisenhower allowed television cameras into a cabinet meeting; once again, the program was carefully planned and the cabinet members were given lines and cues to memorize. On another occasion, Eisenhower appeared in a televised "dialogue" with Secretary of State John Foster Dulles, sitting and listening attentively while Dulles reported to him and the nation on a recent trip abroad.

Shortly after taking office, Eisenhower hired Robert Montgomery, an actor, to be his television adviser. The *Wall Street Journal* quoted a high administration official as saying, "We all suddenly realized we were busy manufacturing a product down here, but nobody was selling it." [59] Eisenhower tried to appear natural and relaxed for the camera, not unlike Roosevelt giving a fireside chat. But his appearances were not consistently effective. A televised Eisenhower budget message, for example, was followed by adverse mail.[60] Eisenhower did not believe television could arouse much interest in what people considered a dull subject, such as inflation. "It is difficult to dramatize the dangers of inflation and while I am willing to resort to television in an effort to talk to the people of the country as a whole, I find it very hard, even using that media, to get much coverage or interest." [61]

But where the president's activities or those of his administration lent themselves to news coverage that would inspire favorable public opinion, television cameras were almost sure to be present. Eisenhower's "peace trip" to Italy, India, Greece, France, and Spain in 1959 was carefully arranged to produce television films of massive crowds welcoming Eisenhower as a hero.

Secretary of State Dulles traveled to foreign countries accompanied by television and radio aides who arranged arrival and departure statements and news conferences and encouraged the networks to attend. When such places as Guatemala and Indochina became important in American foreign policy, a Dulles press conference or speech was often the only available source of news about the place.[62] Dulles also occasionally attempted to shut off news obtained from other sources. After CBS rebroadcast a shortwave report from inside China, the State Department persuaded CBS Chairman William Paley that further reports would not be in the public interest, and he canceled them, despite protests from broadcasters Edward R. Murrow and Eric Sevareid. Subsequent administrations have also had recourse to news blackouts on occasion. No other branch of government, and certainly not the opposition party, has the power to turn news on and off on subjects other than its own activities. By the end of Eisenhower's first term, the executive branch employed nearly seven thousand information experts, almost twice as many as the Truman administration had employed.[63]

Preparing for the national convention in 1956, the Democratic National Committee decided to present a film as a portion of the keynote address and asked Edward R. Murrow to suggest a narrator for the film. Murrow proposed Senator John F. Kennedy as his first choice and Senator Edmund Muskie as his second.[64] The committee then chose Kennedy to narrate the film, which was shown not only to convention delegates but also on the ABC and NBC television networks. This exposure may have helped promote Kennedy's own nomination four years later.

Kennedy was to live television what Roosevelt was to radio. In less than three years in office, he made nine television reports to the nation, a higher yearly rate than that of the Roosevelt fireside chats. His was a natural television talent. His aide, Theodore Sorensen, wrote, "Kennedy's character could be felt in every word." [65] Had he lived, Kennedy might well have demonstrated the full potential of presidential television for creating a favorable presidential image and support for administration policies.

Like Roosevelt, Kennedy came to office over significant newspaper opposition. His press secretary, Pierre Salinger, early in the administration perceived that by using television

Kennedy might bypass the newspapers and reach to the people directly.[66] At Salinger's suggestion, President Kennedy initiated live television coverage of the presidential press conference. Salinger has written:

> My advice was that JFK, the third White House occupant of the television age, be the first to open his press conferences to live coverage by the TV networks. Today, no one blinks at the prospect of the most powerful head of state in the world exposing himself to free and often hostile questions before an audience of many millions and with no possibility of censorship. But in 1960 my proposal was a radical departure from tradition, and the reaction was swift and violent. I had to contend with strong disagreement among JFK's closest advisors, much head shaking in the State Department, and a near riot among the White House correspondents.[67]

James Reston called this advice "the goofiest idea since the hula hoop" [68] and Bill Lawrence accused Salinger of plunging "deeper and deeper into matters about which you know nothing." [69] But the television networks were enthusiastic, and Salinger found "there was . . . no question that TV was willing to preempt millions of dollars in commercial time to carry the press conferences." [70] And carry them free.

Salinger aimed for widespread coverage. Constituents were urged to complain to their local stations if they did not carry the conferences; congressional press secretaries were asked to encourage broadcasts in their districts.[71] According to Sorensen, the press conferences were intended "to inform and impress the public more than the press," and televising them "provided a direct communication with the voters which no newspaper could alter by interpretation or omission." [72] Most of Kennedy's press conferences attracted large television audiences. The first conference he gave was seen by 65 million people.[73] A survey taken in 1962 showed that most people liked and approved of the programs and that 90 percent of those polled had seen or heard at least part of one.[74]

Kennedy began each conference with an opening statement intended to provide a focus for the reporters' questions and to push pending legislation before the great audience.[75] Salinger often saw to it that the attending journalists were primed with questions the president wanted to answer. In any case, Kennedy was always thoroughly prepared for questions. Before each press conference, the press secretaries of the various executive departments submitted to the White House a list of questions reporters might ask. Kennedy went over them with his staff, absorbing facts and figures to use in reply.[76]

As a result the broadcasts lacked spontaneity. Elmer E. Cornwell called the conferences "productions, far closer to a Hollywood epic" than to the press conferences of years past.[77] In fact, as Washington reporter Jules Witcover later pointed out, the press conference is firmly under the president's control: "The conference has its roots in tradition, not in the Constitution or any lesser law, and if it 'belongs' to anyone, it is to the President. . . . He can use it, abuse it, or dispense with it altogether." [78] Some reporters grumbled about the roles to which they were consigned in JFK's productions; secretly, most of them enjoyed participating. For as Arthur Schlesinger, Jr. has observed, a Kennedy press conference was a "superb show, always gay, often exciting, relished by the reporters and by the television audience." [79]

The most serious criticism of the presidential press conference as it developed under Presidents Kennedy, Johnson, and Nixon was that most questions had little or no follow-up. A reporter might ask a question about troop withdrawal from Vietnam; the president would reply briefly; then, instead of probing troop withdrawal deeper, the next reporter might ask a question on tax reform. A *Nation* article by Ted Lewis complained that press conferences "were rapidly becoming a way of extracting only a great deal of superficial information." [80] Because he was the president, and because therefore no one would be rude to him, he could shut off a hard question with "no comment" or with evasion. To avoid follow-up questions, he could abruptly turn to questioners on the other side of the room or "filibuster" with long-winded answers that ate up time.

Like Eisenhower, Kennedy relied on negotiations with the informal three-network committee to clear television time for press conferences and addresses. The networks carried nineteen Kennedy speeches live.[81] Kennedy also sat for informal, lengthy interviews that were filmed for later television use. He was interviewed by Eleanor Roosevelt for educational television, by Bill Lawrence for ABC, by Walter Cronkite for CBS. He developed what has become known as the "conversation" with a president, a televised interview in which the president converses with from one to four network correspondents. On December 17, 1962, all the networks carried a "conversation" among Kennedy and TV correspondents from each of the networks, broadcast live from the president's office. Salinger called this performance "the most dramatic of JFK's appearances. Never before had the American public had such an intimate glimpse of a President: his personality, his mind at work, his sense of history—and his sense of humor." [82] But like the press conferences, the "conversation" was largely controlled by the president.

Kennedy created yet another television innovation when he allowed ABC cameras to follow him as he and Robert Kennedy discussed how to deal with resistance to integration in Alabama, an attempt at presidential *cinema vérité* unlike the staged Eisenhower cabinet meetings, intended to give the public the impression of having access, through television, to the president, rather than the reverse.

President Kennedy's administration, like that of his predecessor, also manufactured and manipulated television news. Following the lead of Eisenhower and Dulles, and foreshadowing President Nixon's use of television during his history-making

China visit years later, Kennedy's trips to Europe in 1961 and 1963 were carefully planned for news effect. Films of his speeches and the crowds that attended them were flown to the United States by jet in time for the evening news. And on more than one occasion, the press accused the Kennedy administration of deliberately withholding or timing the release of important news. Following the Bay of Pigs invasion of Cuba, Kennedy was heavily attacked by the press for unnecessary secrecy and for official distortions of fact, if not outright lies.

Kennedy used television effectively in leading the country through the Berlin tension in 1961 and the Cuban missile showdown in 1962—and during domestic tension over desegregation in Mississippi and Alabama. Of the nine Kennedy televised "reports to the nation" more than half were devoted to crises. In his October 22, 1962, disclosure that the presence of Soviet missiles had been detected in Cuba, Kennedy announced his chosen policy—a naval blockade against shipments of Russian weapons to Cuba—and sold it to the country: "The path we have chosen for the present is full of hazards, as all paths are, but is the one most consistent with our character and courage as a nation and our commitments around the world." [83] His speech was intended not only to inform and unify the American people but also to convince the Soviet Union and Cuba of the firmness of his position. The newspaper press pool that was allowed into the president's office during his speech included, by design, the Washington correspondent of Tass, the Soviet news agency. That same evening, ten radio stations along the U.S. East Coast broadcast the president's address in Spanish for reception in Cuba.

Although there was sentiment in the Congress and the country, on the one hand, for an invasion of Cuba and, on the other hand, for a more conciliatory approach, neither position was able to attract significant support after Kennedy made his television address. Adlai Stevenson's televised speeches at the

United Nations Security Council helped to solidify support for Kennedy's policy. Stevenson's arraignment of the Soviet representative was a memorable moment in the history of presidential television: "You are in the courtroom of world opinion right now, and you can answer 'Yes or No.' . . . I am prepared to wait for my answer until hell freezes over." During the UN phase of the missile crisis, while Kennedy and Khrushchev were locked in secret negotiations, the only voice that could speak publicly for the United States was Stevenson's. In speaking on television, Stevenson compensated for a president's rare inability to appear himself when engaged in sensitive negotiation.

Kennedy did not allow cabinet meetings to be televised. But in February 1963, when Republican Senator Kenneth Keating charged that many Russian missiles still remained in Cuba, Kennedy had a Department of Defense expert go on television to review aerial photographs, which he interpreted as indicating conclusively that the Cuban missile bases had been dismantled; the broadcast closed with a statement by the Secretary of Defense. The missile rumors quickly abated.[84]

Members of Kennedy's family appeared on television from time to time while he was in the White House. One of the most successful of these appearances was the hour-long tour of the White House led by Jacqueline Kennedy on network television in February 1962. Since then the televised White House tour led by a member of the president's family has become a tradition.

The television coverage of President Kennedy's funeral was enormous. The whole nation watched chiefs of state from around the world walk through the White House gate and down the street to the church; the whole nation saw the cortege with its riderless horse and Green Berets; the whole nation heard the muffled drums. Television made the nation's grief a source of unity.

A few days later, Lyndon Johnson made his first formal television appearance as president, addressing a joint session of Congress. The next day, Thanksgiving, the networks carried President Johnson's speech from the White House. In both speeches, Johnson emphasized continuity and, by using television, was able to convey the continuity of government to the American people.

Johnson, like Kennedy, regarded his role in the televised press conference as reaching the people with what he wanted to say rather than discharging an obligation to expose himself to hard questioning. Since the more he talked the less time the reporters had for questions, Johnson often used conferences to make long, routine announcements. Johnson once explained to a TV journalist that he had not held a press conference lately, because he "didn't have any announcements to make." When the journalist pointed out that the purpose of the news conference was to elicit presidential answers and not presidential announcements, the president's expression is said to have soured.[85]

During Johnson's first year in office he appeared on television more often than President Kennedy had in three years; in two years, he appeared more often than Eisenhower had in eight; in 1965, he appeared no less than thirty-six times on live television. He was, indeed, an almost compulsive communicator. In March 1964, *Time* reported that "in the course of a single breathtaking, nerve-shaking, totally impossible week, the 36th President of the United States made nearly two dozen speeches, traveled 2,983 miles, held three press conferences, appeared on national television three times, was seen in person by almost a quarter of a million people." [86]

Johnson often refused to disclose the subject of his broadcasts in advance. Fred Friendly, former president of CBS News, recalls one such unexplained request from the White

House for a segment of Sunday evening prime time worth about $120,000 to each network. Friendly feared that the president "wanted to talk about postal reform or agriculture," topics of little interest to the national prime-time audience. CBS decided to carry the broadcast live, although the other networks did not, and Johnson made an important address on the Dominican Republic.[87]

But in 1964, his demand for prime time for an address that proved to be an announcement of settlement of a railroad labor dispute raised "a serious ethical question for the networks," according to CBS's William Small. "There is no question but that the networks would have used far less [of the Johnson announcement] if they had had opportunity to edit the appearance." [88] In this instance, the networks had received the presidential request for time at 6:23 P.M. Twenty minutes later, in the midst of the network evening news program, Johnson arrived at CBS studios in Washington and asked to begin his announcement immediately.

To accommodate Johnson's desire for instant access to network television and to avoid further impromptu presidential visits to their studios, the networks spent about $250,000 to convert a small theater in the east wing of the White House into a presidential television studio, fully staffed and equipped with three cameras that were kept "warm" for immediate use.[89]

Johnson did not hesitate to go on television at whatever hour he wanted, often disregarding the wishes of the networks. In April 1965, he again interrupted the network evening newscasts with a six-minute appeal for a truce in the Dominican Republic. The president timed his statement to begin shortly after the CBS and NBC news programs began; they carried it live, and ABC taped it and carried it later. On another occasion, Johnson requested a 9:30 P.M. all-network television appearance. Hoping not to disrupt evening audience patterns, the networks asked him to wait until one minute past ten o'clock. But the president decided he was ready to make his announcement and went ahead at 9:55. Instead of the last few minutes of "Bonanza" many of the nation's viewers saw an impatient president. On another occasion, Johnson demonstrated another aspect of the presidential call on television when he suggested in an afternoon conversation with reporters that the networks should provide time for his secretaries of State and Defense to discuss the Vietnam War. Two days later, Dean Rusk and Robert McNamara appeared on a special one-hour edition of "Meet the Press."

Johnson was also the first president to sign bills into law on live national television—a Vietnam appropriations bill, Medicare, a voting rights bill, and an immigration bill. One hundred days after taking office, borrowing a Kennedy technique, Johnson had a "conversation" with the press. He held a second one in December 1967. Both "conversations" were taped, and after the first ten minutes the tape was stopped and replayed so that the president could make sure that he looked his best. He also insisted on editing the tape. The estimated audiences for these two "conversations" were 38 million and 52 million people respectively.[90]

Like Kennedy, Eisenhower, and Truman, Johnson used radio as well as television to reach the public; his televised press conferences, addresses, and "conversations" were also carried on the major radio networks. And like those of his predecessors, President Johnson's cabinet members went on television and radio to promote his policies.

In keeping with the practice of predecessors, Johnson's family made television appearances intended to complement the president's own television efforts. His wife and two daughters participated in a number of informal television interviews during Johnson's five years in the White House. The weddings of Luci Baines Johnson in 1966 and of Lynda Bird Johnson the following year received extensive television coverage on all three networks. Luci's Texas-sized wedding festivities for seven hundred guests were carried live for three hours on ABC, CBS, and NBC, and each network later showed thirty minutes of taped highlights during prime time. Lynda's simpler White House wedding the next year received thirty minutes of live and taped coverage by NBC, thirty minutes of prime-time taped highlights on ABC, and newscast coverage on CBS.

Johnson devoted much energy to presidential television. When told that his appearance was not pleasing to viewers, Johnson "tried contact lenses, face make-up, electronic prompting devices, everything short of plastic surgery to improve his television image." [91] He frequently called reporters or networks himself to complain they had treated him unfairly. He had three television receivers installed in the White House and monitored the networks regularly. When he traveled abroad, television aides carefully created scenes that would have news appeal. For better crowd shots, the presidential bubbletop limousine was flown around the world at considerable expense. In some cases, radio reports about his foreign visits actually were taped before the events took place.[92] At home he played with his dogs and attended rocket launchings for the television cameras. By November 1965, a Republican member of Congress was moved to call him "a master of news management" and, as such, a threat to the survival of the Republican party.[93] Yet, perhaps because his many television appearances were not successful in creating an image capable of withstanding public opposition to his Vietnam policies, Johnson's political power waned and he decided against seeking reelection.

Richard Milhous Nixon took office in 1969 with more television experience than any previous president. His career had been marked by stunning television successes, such as his famous "Checkers Speech," and by the disasters of the 1960 debates with John Kennedy and the televised "last press conference" after losing the California gubernatorial campaign in 1962. As Nixon himself told the National Association of Broadcasters, "Certainly I am the world's living expert on what television can do for a candidate, and what it can do to a candidate." [94] By now he may also be the world's greatest expert on what television can do for and to an incumbent president.

Richard Nixon and television broke onto the national scene at about the same time, in the late 1940s. Nixon made his first appearance on national television in 1948 during hearings on Communists in government held by the Un-American Activities Committee of the U.S. House of Representatives. He was then a thirty-five-year-old first-term congressman. The committee's hearings made front page news when Whittaker Chambers, a senior editor of *Time* magazine, testified that he had belonged to the Communist party from 1925 to 1938. Chambers identified others as Communists whose assignment, he said, had been to infiltrate the government.[95] Among those he named was Alger Hiss, a former State Department official who had later become president of the Carnegie Endowment for International Peace. Hiss unequivocally and persuasively denied Chambers's charges, but Congressman Nixon was unconvinced.

During the weeks that followed, the newspapers reported the ongoing exchange of charges and denials between Chambers and Hiss, hinted at dramatic disclosures to come, and gave a favorable account of Nixon's role in the proceedings. The confrontation between Hiss and Chambers before the full committee, shown on national television, gave Nixon his first taste of television-induced fame.

Four years after the Hiss case broke, television again served Nixon well when, as junior senator from California and Republican nominee for vice president on the Eisenhower ticket, he made his celebrated "Checkers Speech." In mid-September

1952, word of a "secret Nixon fund" contributed by wealthy Californians had begun to appear in the newspapers, raising the question of whether Senator Nixon had accepted money in exchange for political favors. These newspaper reports were followed by editorials demanding that Nixon resign from the ticket. With minimal support from Eisenhower and amid increasing public clamor, Nixon and his advisers decided to take his case to the national television audience.

All across the country people were speculating as to whether or not Nixon was going to resign. He made the broadcast in NBC's El Capitan Theater in Los Angeles during prime evening television time. The speech was carried on 64 NBC-TV stations, 194 CBS radio stations, and most of the Mutual Broadcasting System's 560 stations. NBC later estimated a viewing audience of 25 million; some 40 million radios were tuned in.[96]

Nixon began by addressing the "slush fund" charges, declaring that the fund was neither secret nor for his personal use. He then attacked the records of the Democratic candidates, warned about Communist strength in Washington under Democratic administrations, and praised Eisenhower. But what the speech is best remembered for is Nixon's passionate assertion that he would never make his children give up their cocker spaniel, Checkers, a gift from Nixon supporters.

The slush fund charges were quickly forgotten. The public was carried away by the sentimental and patriotic passages of the speech and by Nixon's attacks on the Truman administration and on the Democratic ticket. And newspaper editorials were drowned out by the emotional impact of television.

It was perhaps the most brilliant political use that had ever been made of the mass media. The speech not only saved Nixon's political career but also spread his fame far beyond his California political base. Its dramatic demonstration of the influence of television on voters added a whole new dimension to political campaigning. Immediately after the broadcast, some two million letters and wires poured into Republican headquarters, urging, "Keep Nixon on the ticket." Many newspapers, such as the *New York Herald Tribune,* which had earlier suggested that Nixon withdraw, came out in support of the television audience's decision: Thumbs Up.[97] (Not all commentators were favorably impressed, however—Walter Lippmann was disturbed by the prospect of "mob law by modern electronics." [98])

Like millions of other Americans, Eisenhower watched the telecast and saw his own skepticism turn to approval. At the conclusion of the speech, he turned to GOP National Chairman Arthur Summerfield and said, "Well, you got your money's worth." When Nixon flew to join the Eisenhower campaign in West Virginia, the general bounded up the stairs of the plane, embraced Nixon, and said, "You're my boy." [99] For the remainder of the campaign, Nixon attracted large television audiences. "He had become a star." [100]

Nixon returned to nationwide television in 1956 when, as vice president, he successfully campaigned with President Eisenhower for a second term. An Eisenhower aide urged administration campaigners to "give Dick Nixon a boost in their speeches," [101] and they made a concerted effort to change Nixon's image from that of a gloves-off fighter to that of a mature and responsible statesman, ready and able to step into the presidency. According to a study of the campaign, this effort met with some success and "television and radio helped to set [Nixon's] new image." [102]

Near the end of his second term as vice president, Nixon looked back on the role played by television in the Eisenhower campaigns:

> Television is not so effective now as it was in 1952. The novelty has worn off. There is a very early point of diminishing returns in using television. Both parties did too much of it in the 1956

campaign. People probably get tired of seeing favorite programs thrown off for political speeches. I believe in personal appearances and think the personal touch is still the most effective way of campaigning. . . .[103]

Yet the 1960 presidential campaign between Vice President Richard Nixon and Senator John F. Kennedy will always be remembered for the "Great Debates," four live telecast debates that brought the two major candidates face to face into the homes of more than half the nation's population. In the "Great Debates," for the first time the Democratic and Republican presidential nominees appeared simultaneously and nationwide on all networks. During the 1948 Oregon presidential primary, Republican Governors Harold Stassen and Thomas Dewey had debated on radio. And in 1952, televised debates between Eisenhower and Stevenson had been proposed.[104] But the two major party candidates had never appeared together on nationwide television, at least in part because Section 315 of the Federal Communications Act requires that a broadcaster offer time to all candidates for an office if he provides time to any one candidate for that office. Under Section 315, if a broadcaster made time available to a major party candidate, not only the candidate of the other major party but the candidates of all the minor parties—ranging in 1960 from Orval Faubus of the National States Rights Party to Syman Gould of the American Vegetarian Party—could request, and would be entitled to receive, "equal opportunities" on the station. Under these conditions, the broadcast industry had been unwilling to promote a debate between the major candidates. But in 1960, Congress temporarily suspended the equal-time provision for presidential and vice presidential candidates. Social scientists, politicians, and broadcasters are still disputing the significance of the debates. The candidates themselves, however, were in complete agreement: Nixon stated, "Looking back now on all four of them there can be no question but that Kennedy had gained more from the debates than I," [105] and Kennedy admitted, "We wouldn't have had a prayer without that gadget [television]." [106]

The election was the closest in modern history. Kennedy won by only 112,000 votes out of more than 68 million cast. He got 49.7 percent of the vote, Nixon 49.6 percent. Exactly how many voters were influenced by the televised debates is unknown. But most students of the subject agree that in one sense, almost from the moment the first debate began, Kennedy won; he entered the debates as a young junior senator little known outside Massachusetts, whereas Nixon had been vice president of the United States for eight years, but in the debates they appeared on the screen as equals.

Some 75 million people, more than voted in the election, saw the first debate on September 26. The domestic issues touched upon during the hour-long show (reduction of the federal debt, raising teachers' salaries, Kennedy's maturity and fitness for the presidency) have long since been forgotten by most viewers. What they remembered was that Nixon appeared "tense, almost frightened, at turns glowering and, occasionally, haggard-looking to the point of sickness." [107] The lighting, the set, Nixon's weight loss due to a recent hospitalization, his lack of makeup —all contributed to an unattractive television image. The camera was more flattering to Kennedy. Nixon later commented: "At the conclusion of our postmortem, I recognized the basic mistake I had made. I had concentrated too much on substance and not enough on appearance." [108]

He did not repeat this mistake. But, although in subsequent debates his staff paid great attention to details of dress, lighting, and makeup, the damage had already been done. Radio listeners called the first debate a draw, but television viewers perceived that first image of Nixon and it could not be erased. Nixon himself wrote: "One bad camera angle on television can have far more effect on the election outcome than a major mistake in writing a speech which is then picked up and criticized by columnists and editorial writers." [109]

Two years later, when Nixon ran for governor of California, he scheduled seven three-hour telethons and overwhelmed his opponent, incumbent Edmund G. "Pat" Brown, in a television debate.[110] Brown, nevertheless, won reelection decisively. On the day after the election, Nixon appeared on television in what he called his "last press conference." Bitterly disappointed by the election results, and physically exhausted, he lashed out at the newspaper reporters who had covered the campaign: "You won't have Nixon to kick around any more." He also gave broadcasters resounding praise: "I think it's time that our great newspapers have at least the same objectivity, the same fullness of coverage that television has. And I can only thank God for television and radio for keeping the newspapers a little more honest." [111]

Nixon moved to New York and joined a law firm and from this base he slowly built up new support within his bitterly divided party. After the overwhelming defeat of Barry Goldwater in 1964, the possibility of a Nixon candidacy in 1968 became ever more likely. By 1967, he had a winning strategy. It represented a new approach to mass communications. In the old days of campaigning, the candidate had tried to see in person as many of the voters as possible—at political rallies, train stations, banquets, factory gates, and parades. But his real objective was to be seen by as many voters as possible. The best medium for access to a mass audience is television. County fairs and ticker-tape parades were reduced to colorful settings in which the candidate might appear to advantage on the television screen. The effort was directed not at the event itself but at the image it would convey to voters far removed from the event. The day was past when the big event of the campaign was the mammoth Saturday night political rally, aimed at the precinct captains in the hall and at the Sunday morning newspaper headlines. What mattered now was a visit to a photogenic background to provide a film clip for the seven o'clock evening news. And if the candidate was campaigning in California, he must create his television event early in the morning in order to make the evening news back East where the news broadcasts originate, three hours ahead of California time. In Richard Nixon's 1968 campaign, and in innumerable campaigns since, television—not the newspapers or the immediate audience—has been the target. For in 1968, television reached virtually every home in the United States.

The Nixon strategy in 1968 was by no means an indiscriminate pursuit of any and all television exposure. Nixon's campaign staff carefully and rigidly controlled every detail of his television appearances.[112] In fact, Nixon rejected all invitations to appear on network shows from early 1967 until late October 1968. The 1960 Great Debates had taught him a bitter lesson. He would take no more chances with programs that might show him in an unfavorable light, literally or figuratively. He would not appear on interview shows and risk potentially embarrassing questions. Control was the key, and the Nixon men maintained tight control almost to the end. And in 1968 Nixon did not have to engage in televised debates with the Democratic nominee, Vice President Hubert Humphrey. The equal-time provision of the Federal Communications Act was again in effect, and Republican leaders in Congress had no desire to see it suspended. (Neither had their Democratic colleagues, four years earlier, when Lyndon Johnson was the front runner.) The GOP had money to buy television time and their candidate was already well known; the party would not throw away this advantage as it had in 1960.

As a concession to spontaneity, Nixon's managers revived the "Citizens Press Conference" format introduced by President Eisenhower in 1956. A panel of seven to nine citizens, chosen by the Nixon staff to represent a desired mix of voters, asked

Nixon unrehearsed questions. Only at the end of the campaign did Nixon, disturbed by signs of growing Democratic strength, appear on CBS's "Face the Nation" and NBC's "Meet the Press," add ten evening radio broadcasts to his schedule, put a Nixon biography on daytime television for housewives, and buy time for not one but two election-eve telethons.

Nixon won the election with only 43.4 percent of the total vote. Humphrey received 42.7 percent of the votes cast, and third-party candidate George Wallace got 13.5 percent. No one can say how much television contributed to Nixon's narrow victory, but Democrats complained bitterly about the money he had spent on television and about their own poverty.

President Nixon thus came to the White House with vast television experience. In office he has explored the potential of the medium in governance and politics as Roosevelt explored that of radio. He has become an innovator in presidential television and has made far more extensive and varied use of it than his predecessors.

The Nixon White House staff has included more experts from the worlds of broadcasting, advertising, and public relations than ever before. Among the president's aides have been a former newspaper editor, television news producer, advertising account executive, television production expert, broadcast news reporter, and broadcast program manager. The president also introduced a special Office of Communications for the Executive Branch, responsible for maintaining the administration's public image on the nation's television screens. Eyeing the many members of Nixon's staff with media experience, FCC Commissioner Nicholas Johnson has charged that "what emerges is the overwhelming impression of an Administration whose fixed focus is on the little glass screen." [113]

President Nixon also has been an innovator in use of television in prime time—the hours between 7:00–11:00 P.M.—when the largest number of people watch television. During his

administration, presidential television nearly became synony-
mous with prime time. In his first eighteen months in the White
House, Nixon appeared during the prime viewing hours as
frequently as Presidents Eisenhower, Kennedy, and Johnson
combined during the first eighteen months of their respective
terms.[114] The CBS network calculates that during his first thirty-nine months in office, President Nixon made thirty-one special prime-time appearances, compared to twenty-four similar
appearances by President Johnson in five years, ten by President Kennedy in three years, and twenty-three by President Eisenhower in eight years.[115]

The increased use of prime time is a significant development
in presidential television because of the marked difference in
audience size between prime-time and non-prime-time appearances. For example, President Nixon's 1970 State of the Union
message was broadcast live at 12:30 P.M. (EST) and reached
about 22.5 million people; [116] his 1971 State of the Union
speech was broadcast at 9:00 P.M. and reached 54.4 million people. The audience more than doubled in size largely because the
president went to prime time.[117] Research by CBS concludes
that as a result of the move of presidential television to prime
time the typical television viewer saw President Nixon for almost 50 percent more time than he saw President Kennedy during the first eighteen months of their administrations.[118]

Another Nixon innovation was the live "conversation." Presidents Kennedy and Johnson had participated in discussions
with newsmen that were filmed or taped for later broadcast. Although President Nixon added the element of excitement of a
live broadcast, he retained control. As one network newsman
observed, the "President is pretty well in the driver's seat during these transactions." [119] The "conversation" of January 4,
1971, which marked the end of Nixon's first two years in the
White House, was described in *Time* magazine as a "public relations triumph for Richard Nixon." The format, *Time* ob-

served, precluded hard questions and gave the president a
chance to present his views to an audience of 55 million people.[120] Like his predecessors, President Nixon found the networks willing to provide him with access to this audience.
Broadcasting magazine reported that White House aides "told
networks last week [the] President would be available . . . and
networks promptly began making arrangements." [121]

In addition to his own innovations, President Nixon has
made deft use of television techniques developed by other presidents. Lacking the remarkable charisma of John Kennedy, and
perhaps with an eye to some of the unimpressive showings of
Presidents Eisenhower and Johnson, Nixon decreased the frequency of televised presidential news conferences. After his
first months in office, those few conferences he did hold were
moved from their traditional midday time slot, designed so earlier presidents could reach the evening papers, to the larger audience in prime time. As in the past, the prime-time news conferences are carried live by the three commercial television
networks under a "network pool" arrangement. The Washington news bureaus of ABC, CBS, and NBC provide equipment
and camera crews on a rotating basis, and all three networks
pick up the signal for simultaneous broadcast. The White
House approves technical details of lighting, voice amplifica-
tion, seating arrangements, and set.

In a typical broadcast press conference, President Nixon an-
swered fifteen to twenty-five questions posed by a handful of
the two hundred or so reporters present in the East Room of
the White House. He used no notes and usually stood alone in
front of the bright blue curtains without a podium. Occasionally
he had an opening statement or announcement, but more often
he plunged right in and pointed to one of the two wire service
correspondents, who traditionally had the honor of asking the
first question. News conference questions covered a wide variety of topics but tended to stress foreign policy and national se-

curity matters, areas in which President Nixon always had made a particularly strong showing. In June 1971, the president reported that a survey of questions asked at all his news conferences since taking office showed that 85 percent of them dealt with foreign policy or national security; only 15 percent concerned domestic issues.[122]

The president's evening news conferences were regularly viewed by 40 or 50 million people across the country, more than 100,000 times the number of people who could fit into the East Room to see them in person. The conferences received advance newspaper publicity, often on the front page or in the television section. President Nixon told reporters at one conference, "I consider a press conference as going to the country. I find that these conferences are rather well covered by the country, both by television, as they are today, and also by the members of the press." [123]

During and immediately after the 1972 presidential campaign, and at the start of his second term in 1973, President Nixon made little use of television. In the campaign, he was ahead; why take risks, especially with a Vietnam ceasefire in the balance? [124] After the election, he had the mandate of a landslide victory; again, why take risks—and again, Vietnam. However, as confidence in his administration fell with the revelation in 1973 that the White House had been involved in bugging the Democratic party's Watergate headquarters and in other secret activities, Nixon turned to television, as he had in past crises, to defend himself. His attempt to explain the Watergate scandal was seen by almost 80 million television viewers.

During the Nixon administration, including even the 1972 election and postelection period, the president's use of radio—radio alone, without television—reemerged as it had not for some years. President Nixon, a former debater and lawyer, has always been an effective speaker, but at times, as in the 1960 Great Debates, his picture on television has served him ill.

Radio presents no such problem—his face is missing, his voice is as effective as ever. Moreover, a radio program can be recorded under far less pressure than a television program. Again, President Nixon has feared overexposure on television; radio solves that problem.[125] And when he makes a network radio-only speech, newspapers will report that he "spoke to the nation" and will cover the substance of his speech fully. Finally, radio-only broadcasts allow the president to direct messages to particular audiences. Many of his radio addresses have been devoted to economic or agricultural issues and have been broadcast during daytime hours when the audience can be expected to be housewives concerned with rising food costs, unemployed workers or farm workers not confined to regular office hours.

During his first term, President Nixon made particularly effective use of broadcasting through a series of preemptive television addresses about his policy on Vietnam. Although a great many factors have influenced public opinion on this issue —certainly the most complex and volatile foreign policy controversy in many years—presidential television played a significant role in maintaining public support for the president's position and in enabling him to withstand congressional attempts to limit his discretion in dealing with Vietnam developments.

The president delivered his first television address about Vietnam after four months in office, calling for peace through the phased withdrawal of both American and North Vietnamese troops fron South Vietnam. But dissatisfaction with the administration's Vietnam policies was growing and the dissenters, too, capitalized on the media. In October 1969, "moratorium" demonstrations were held in cities and towns across the country; young and old alike wore black arm bands to school or work to express antiwar sentiment. One month later, crowds estimated at between 200,000 and 500,000 demonstrated in Washington against the war. Protesting voices were heard again in May 1970, after American troops widened the war into Cambodia. Emotions escalated along with the distant military activity as television newsclips showed the president calling young protestors "bums." Four students at Ohio's Kent State University were killed as troops fired into a crowd of antiwar demonstrators. Opposition to the president's policies mounted. Every night television showed films of the war and news about growing public questioning of the government's policies.

On Capitol Hill, opponents of the president's Southeast Asian policies began to move. Senators and congressmen proposed legislation setting a deadline for the American presence in Cambodia and restricting the president's freedom to continue military action outside South Vietnam. What the president himself described as "an unprecedented barrage of criticism," [126] was duly covered by television.

But television also became the medium through which President Nixon mounted his counterattack. During the six months between November 1969 and April 1971, he preempted evening television time on no fewer than seven occasions to ask for support of administration policies and to slow the momentum of the peace movement among the public and on Capitol Hill. In November 1969, before an audience of 72 million people (9 million more than had voted for him and Humphrey combined), the president argued that dissent within the country over U.S. policy in Southeast Asia damaged the cause of eventual peace in Vietnam:

> And so tonight—to you, the great silent majority of my fellow Americans—I ask for your support. . . . The more support I can have from the American people, the sooner [peace can be won]; for the more divided we are at home, the less likely the enemy is to negotiate at Paris. Let us be united for peace. Let us also be united against defeat. Because let us understand: North

Vietnam cannot defeat or humiliate the United States. Only Americans can do that.[127]

The following month he addressed a nationwide television audience of 42 million people for five minutes to announce a withdrawal of 50,000 more troops from Vietnam and to repeat requests for support.

In April 1970, more than 60 million people watched the president announce the phased withdrawal of 150,000 more troops, state that "we can now say with confidence that pacification is succeeding," praise the American people for their selflessness, and declare that the United States would not suffer defeat in Vietnam. Ten days later, the president was on the air again, this time with the surprise announcement that American troops were invading Cambodia to capture the "headquarters of the entire Communist military operation" in South Vietnam. (During the weeks that followed, administration spokesmen maintained that the Cambodian operation was achieving its objectives, while critics called it a blunder or a failure.) One month later the president made still another broadcast address on Southeast Asia, this time to deliver an "interim report" on the Cambodian "incursion." He told a television audience of 50 million viewers that the use of troops in Cambodia was "the most successful operation of this long and very difficult war" and reported that "all of our major military objectives have been achieved." He used Defense Department films to illustrate his remarks and concluded with another call for an end to dissent.[128]

The president made another prime-time address on Vietnam in October 1970, reaching more than half of all American homes with television sets tuned in. In a calm and unemotional tone he proposed an immediate cease-fire throughout Indochina, an all-Indochina Peace Conference, the complete withdrawal of all outside forces, and a political settlement to the war. Finally, in prime time on April 7, 1971, the president took to the air to assure the public and Congress that his policy of Vietnamization of the Asian conflict had succeeded.

Most observers believe the Nixon television effort on Vietnam to have been effective. David S. Broder, a *Washington Post* political writer, called it "a devastating use of television." [129] And members of the administration concurred. After Nixon's November 30, 1969, address, Ray Price, one of his speechwriters, said, "Judging by the results, it was the most effective use of TV that's ever been done. You had the massively accelerating peace movement. But after the speech, the balloon just fizzled." [130]

Finding themselves the losers in the war powers debate with the president, members of Congress complained about the effectiveness of presidential television. "The President has used his prime time television series to present his position on the war, to discount the role of Congress in charting a course in Indochina and to ciriticize his Senate opponents and their position on the war." [131] On the basis of this and similar complaints, the Federal Communications Commission found that President Nixon's first five preemptive television addresses had created a definite imbalance in favor of the president in network television's presentation of the Vietnam issue.

The formal address form of presidential television has served President Nixon equally well in other battles with Congress for public support. While his predecessors had signed popular legislation on television hoping to secure support for future legislation, President Nixon made history by being the first chief executive to sign a legislative veto on television. In a ten-minute appearance during prime time, Nixon explained why he opposed an HEW appropriations bill passed by the Congress. He then picked up a pen and signed the veto message, saying his action was "in the vital interest of all Americans in stopping the rise in the cost of living." [132] Vetoing funds for education has obvious political dangers. But as *Broadcasting* magazine noted, television enabled him to explain directly to the American people, without interruption, why he was doing it.[133]

Even during his first term, it was not unusual for President Nixon to discuss Congress and specific legislation in television addresses. In a June 1970 address on economic policy, Nixon suggested that the Congress had been dragging its feet during the last session and might behave irresponsibly during the coming election campaign. He warned the Congress not "to play politics with inflation by passing legislation granting the president standby powers to impose wage and price controls." He said he would not use such powers if they were granted because "they would do more harm than good." He ran through a long list of administration economic proposals on which the Congress had not acted, and four times repeated the sentence, "It is time for the Congress to act." [134] His message was clear: congressional recalcitrance and "politics" were preventing the executive branch from solving the nation's problems.

The opposition political party, like Congress, has borne the brunt of presidential attacks on television. In a number of addresses, President Nixon took issue with the Democratic Party through references to "the old formulas or tired rhetoric of the past," [135] "the policy of the previous administration [that] resulted in our assuming primary responsibility for fighting the war," [136] "the frequent failure to balance the federal budget over the past five years [that] has been the primary cause for unbalancing the family budgets of millions of Americans." [137]

Altogether, in his first thirty-six months in office, President Nixon preempted television programming on all three networks simultaneously to make an announcement, deliver an address, or report on recent events a total of seventeen times. According to Don Oberdorfer, a White House newsman, "the report to the nation . . . has become a major tool of politics and statecraft for the President." [138] In these preemptive appearances, President Nixon logged nearly three and a half hours of prime network time plus an additional hour of non-prime time, and this does not include press conferences, interviews, and other occasions. Comparable blocks of time could cost an advertiser over $2 million. Sold as spot commercials the time could cost $3 million, an amount comparable to the 1969 television advertising budget of American Telephone and Telegraph, Trans World Airlines, or Mobil Oil.[139]

The incumbent president also has made politically effective use of the wide range of less direct forms of presidential television—the interview, the special event appearance, the newsmaking trip, and appearances of political allies. These informal television appearances have enhanced the president's image, which, as all politicians acknowledge, helps reelect leaders or surrounds them with elected allies. Twice, for example, the president chatted informally with Barbara Walters on NBC's popular "Today" show. The second appearance, made at the president's own suggestion, consisted largely of presidential remarks about the role of women in society and the influence of Mrs. Nixon on his career; two-thirds of the viewers of the "Today" show are women. The Democratic National Committee, through its general counsel, Joseph Califano, charged:

> The interview offered the President a unique opportunity to present to the "Today" audience facets of his personality and private life that are seldom revealed to the public. Most of the questions he was asked focused on his family life, the impact of his public career on his family and the role of his wife in the decisions he was required to make as a public official. Throughout the program, questions were asked with the utmost deference, permitting the President to project a highly favorable image.[140]

Similarly, after one of the president's network "conversations," the Democrats charged the president had used his television access "virtually to announce his undisguised intention to seek reelection":

> The bulk of the program was devoted to the President's explanation of his programs and policies in Vietnam. The President

used the occasion of the interview to blame previous Democratic administrations for the tragic conflict in Vietnam, to extol the success of his Vietnamization policies and to claim that the invasions of Cambodia and Laos had been military successes. He also rationalized his opposition to announcing a date for withdrawal of all American forces from Vietnam—a position that is in direct conflict with that of the Senate and House Democratic Caucuses and of the DNC Policy Council.[141]

The telecast of President Nixon speaking to the students at Kansas State University made his audience's enthusiastic response clearly visible to television viewers. And the president became part of one of America's favorite pastimes when he was interviewed as a sports fan during half-time of the telecast of the 1969 Texas-Arkansas football game and when he delivered a televised half-time message during a professional football game the following year. He shared the audience for man's first step on the moon by placing a televised "phone call" to the men on the moon; 125 million television viewers were watching, probably the most people ever to see and hear a political leader at one time. And, in the tradition of his predecessors, he has been televised wishing for peace while lighting the national Christmas tree in Washington and acclaiming the accomplishments of the past year in the annual State of the Union message.

An occasional television glimpse of the president's family may also help the presidential image. Like those of Lynda and Luci Johnson, Tricia Nixon's wedding reception received television coverage. (The ceremony itself was not shown on television.) Excerpts of the afternoon and evening festivities were shown live and then rebroadcast on late-night news programs across the country. Viewers saw the beaming president, the fairytale-princess bride, dancing, and cake-cutting at the White House. What is usually a private family celebration became a national event.

The Nixon White House has encouraged members of the administration to appear on television (see Appendix A, Table 8). The White House staff has served as a go-between for government officials in their dealings with the networks, and the Office of Communications has attempted to oversee the public image of the entire administration. It has monitored newscasts and newspapers to see where the administration's image needed to be corrected and has orchestrated the television appearances of administration leaders. Herbert Klein, director of the office has said:

> Members of my office and myself work in constant liaison with the departments of government, ranging from cabinet departments to the smaller departments which from time to time assume major importance. . . . Our attitude is that we want the cabinet officers to be in various parts of the country explaining to the American people what happens in their departments. We want them on television as much as possible.[142]

An Office of Management and Budget estimate placed the executive branch public relations bill for fiscal year 1971— excluding the public relations outlay of the White House—at $164 million. Of this sum, $8.2 million, more than the entire annual television advertising budget of the Ford Motor Company or Campbell's Soups, was specifically earmarked for broadcasting purposes.[143]

Perhaps the most remarkable presidential television production of the Nixon administration was the president's visit to China in February 1972. The occasion, the television networks, and the White House itself combined to produce what one White House staffer called "one of the most exciting events in TV history." [144] At White House urging, the Chinese hosts agreed to live television coverage of the Nixon entourage via satellite communications. Three huge cargo planes transported a twenty-ton "portable" transmitting station and fifty tons of additional equipment to China; more than one hundred television technicians, producers, and executives followed.

The networks estimated that their coverage of the president's seven days in China cost them between two and three million dollars. This enabled approximately 100 million viewers to see at least some portion of forty-one hours of network coverage.[145] On the day of the president's arrival in China, Washington, D.C., viewers, for example, could watch, on one network alone, special coverage beginning at 6:00 P.M. and continuing until 10:00 A.M. the next day with relatively few interruptions.

As candidates in the 1972 presidential primaries began their media efforts in New Hampshire, the White House sought to maximize the television opportunity offered by the China visit. The president's plane arrived in Peking in prime time. It managed to return to Washington in prime time only by sitting on the ground for nine hours in Anchorage, Alaska. In his opening remarks at his first banquet in Peking, the president referred to the television audience—"more people are seeing and hearing what we say than on any other occasion in the whole history of the world." As President Nixon toured the Great Wall of China, reporter Max Frankel observed that the president showed "by his gaze that he knew the position of every camera emplacement." [146] Upon the president's return, columnist Art Buchwald satirized the saturation telecasting from China by suggesting that since his television set no longer produced only President Nixon, it must be broken:

> It was two days after President Nixon's return from China and the family went into the living room after dinner to watch television.
> My wife turned on the set and said "That's funny. There seems to be something wrong with the TV. I can't get President Nixon on the tube." . . . "I can't understand it," I said, "President Nixon has been coming in loud and clear on prime time every evening. But tonight all I can get is a movie, Dean Martin, and a Lucy rerun." [147]

Television coverage of the China trip made some observers realize the close connection among television, presidential politics, and presidential leadership. Columnist William F. Buckley, Jr., usually a Nixon supporter but opposed to his China policy, commented on the president's motives in taking a trip "for prime time." [148] Correspondent Peter Lisagor suggested that "television became a Presidential accessory," [149] while Hugh Sidey of *Time* said "for the first time I felt I saw a real fusion of the government apparatus with television." [150] President Nixon, however, had but followed the examples of Eisenhower and Dulles, Kennedy and Johnson. Like those who preceded him and those who will succeed him, he used television to advance his policies and his position of leadership.

CHAPTER 3

THE LIMITS
OF THE LAW

IN A SINGLE nine-month period from November 1969 through July 1970, President Nixon preempted network evening television eleven times for televised addresses or press conferences. Of those eleven presidential prime-time appearances, six were devoted largely or completely to his policies in Southeast Asia. During this same period, the president made six appearances at other times in the broadcast day (see Appendix A, Table 7).

His average of two network appearances per month, and particularly his emphasis on prime-time foreign policy addresses, disturbed his political and congressional opponents as well as organizations opposed to the war. All complained they lacked enough access to television to rebut the president's arguments and oppose his leadership. A number of them took their complaints about presidential television to the Federal Communications Commission.

In May 1970, about thirty Yale University law students, professors, and citizens from New Haven, Connecticut, calling themselves the Committee for the Fair Broadcasting of Controversial Issues, filed a complaint at the FCC against stations WTIC-TV, Hartford, and WCBS-TV, New York. They argued that, contrary to the FCC's "fairness doctrine," the stations had failed to provide a fair opportunity for the balanced presentation of views contrary to the president's. A group called the Business Executives Move for Vietnam Peace, representing 2,700 antiwar business executives, filed a similar complaint against the three major networks. About the same time, fourteen U.S. senators formed an Amendment to End the War Committee and complained to the FCC that the president's presentation of his views on television had not been balanced by a presentation of the views of his congressional opponents. The committee also purchased, for $60,000, a half hour on NBC and presented Senators Goodell, McGovern, Hatfield, Hughes, and Church in a program urging viewers to support pending legislation to cut off funds for the Vietnam War. As a result, eleven Senate supporters of the president's policy, led by the Republican national chairman, Senator Robert Dole, complained to the FCC and demanded a free half-hour on NBC to reply.

Meanwhile, the Democratic party tried to buy television time to broadcast spot announcements opposing the president. Unable to do so, the Democratic National Committee (DNC) petitioned the FCC to rule that a broadcaster could not arbitrarily refuse to sell spot time for comment on controversial issues or solicitation of funds. On June 22, 1970, Frank Stanton, president of CBS, offered the DNC chairman, Lawrence O'Brien, twenty-five minutes of free time on CBS to present the DNC's views. Stanton also told O'Brien that CBS would accept paid spots from political parties for fund-raising purposes. His reasons for adopting this policy were, as he saw them, "simple and obvious; we live in a two party system." [1] He planned these twenty-five minutes of free time as the first in a continuing series of CBS programs to be called "The Loyal Opposition"— free prime network time that the major opposition party could use "from time to time during the year" in any way it saw fit.

On July 7 the DNC went on the air. O'Brien used his free time to attack the president not only on the war but on a broad range of issues, including the economy and domestic disharmony. The program reached millions of viewers and was followed on many stations by a paid spot soliciting funds for the DNC. The *New York Times* called the program "a novel television assault" on Nixon. [2]

The Republicans were quick to react. The Republican National Committee (RNC) asked CBS for free time to respond to the Democrats' response to the president. When CBS refused, the RNC filed a complaint at the FCC. Its complaint called "The Loyal Opposition" program "a political attack on the president and his party" rather than a response to the president's speeches on war policy. Therefore, the RNC contended, the program raised a new issue not treated by the president: which political party should hold power? According to the RNC, the network had a duty to seek out an appropriate spokesman to respond to that question. The appropriate spokesman was, of course, the RNC.

CBS insisted it was in compliance with the FCC's fairness doctrine. It pointed out that the president had already spoken many times on television about all the issues raised by the Democrats and that many news and public affairs programs had also presented the Republican viewpoint. Under the circumstances, CBS did not feel that it had been unfair.

All these complaints, by politicians, citizens' groups, and broadcasters resulted in one of the most hectic debates in television history. For when President Nixon repeatedly took to television to discuss his war policy, it suddenly had become clear that neither existing law or FCC regulatory policy took into account the impact of presidential television. A harried FCC official reportedly remarked, "The situation is worse than I have ever seen it before. We are probably going to have more trouble this year than at any time since the Government started regulating broadcasting." [3]

Federal regulation of radio broadcasting dates back to the 1920s, a period of rapid and uncontrolled growth in the radio industry, when interference resulting from stations broadcasting, increasing power, or changing frequencies virtually at will was making it difficult for anyone to be heard. President Calvin Coolidge observed that "the whole service of this most important public function has drifted into such chaos as seems likely, if not remedied, to destroy its great value." [4] Coolidge and Herbert Hoover, his Secretary of Commerce, as well as the radio industry itself, agreed that legislation was essential to bring order to broadcasting. Congress accordingly passed the Radio Act of 1927, which established the present theoretical basis for governmental regulation of broadcasting. The 1927 act established the principle that the airwaves are a natural resource that belongs to the public and can be used by private interests only "if public convenience, interest, or necessity will be served thereby." [5]

Regulation took into account the peculiarities of the broadcast spectrum. A broadcaster transmits signals, by means of radio waves that oscillate at a given frequency, to receivers designed to pick up signals at that frequency. But the spectrum of radio frequencies is limited, which means that the number of broadcasters who may operate in a given area is also limited. For if two broadcasters use the same frequencies, their signals will be received together and will interfere with each other's clear reception. The mammoth interference on the air in the

1920s had made it apparent that not everyone who wished to could engage in broadcasting. Congress determined that those who were to be granted spectrum space must operate as trustees for the rest. It gave the Secretary of Commerce, with the assistance of a Federal Radio Commission, the power to license prospective broadcasters in such a manner as to ensure that stations would be fairly distributed geographically, would operate as trustees for the public, and would serve the public interest.

These principles were carried over into the Communications Act of 1934, which created the Federal Communications Commission to carry out its provisions. They also have been the basis for further delineation of broadcast regulatory theory by the courts. In 1942, the Supreme Court confirmed that because of the scarcity of spectrum space broadcasters do not have a "right" to unregulated use of radio facilities; rather, they can operate only in conformance with the public interest standard as it may be reasonably defined by the FCC. As the Court put it:

> Unlike other modes of expression radio inherently is not available to all. That is its unique characteristic, and that is why, unlike other modes of expression, it is subject to governmental regulation. Because it cannot be used by all, some who wish to use it must be denied. . . . The standard . . . provided for the licensing of stations was the "public interest, convenience or necessity." [6]

The law views the broadcast licensee as a trustee for the community he serves and holds him responsible for making the opinions and voices of the community available to listeners or viewers over his facilities. It is not the broadcaster but the audience that can claim a broadcast "right":

> It is the right of the viewers and listeners, not the right of the broadcasters which is paramount. . . . It is the right of the public to receive suitable access to social, political, esthetic, moral and other ideas and experiences which is crucial here. [7]

Over the years, the FCC has developed and applied specific requirements and policy "doctrines" to protect this right: programming requirements, equal time, fairness, and the political party doctrine. Some of these establish what might be described as a limited "right to access" to the broadcast media for groups or individuals, including candidates and political parties. But none of them really responds to the problems created by presidential television.

As for *programming requirements,* the FCC has established that the grant and renewal of a broadcast license should depend upon the licensee's provision of adequate broadcast service, including a reasonable amount of programming devoted to the discussion of "public issues." [8] Electoral and political issues are among the "public issues" for which a licensee is obligated to provide broadcast exposure. And the FCC has referred specifically to "the needs and interests of the community with respect to political broadcasts." [9] A station that does not broadcast some political programming, either by creating its own or by giving or selling time to political spokesmen, would be showing "some lack of attention to the needs of the area" or "a degree of inattentiveness to matters of local interest." [10]

Although the law now gives the FCC the specific power to revoke a broadcast license for a licensee's failure to allow political *candidates* reasonable access through free or purchased time,[11] there is no similar provision requiring access for party spokesmen who are not candidates. The FCC has declined to create specific political coverage requirements although, according to its general counsel, it could so do legally.[12] In the absence of specific requirements, a recent FCC survey disclosed that news programs constitute between 4.5 percent and 9.0 percent of a television station's broadcast time (depending upon station size), and public affairs programs constitute between 2.2

percent and 3.0 percent.[13] One reputable private survey claims that in the 1970–71 television season prime-time news and public affairs programs made up only 2 percent of total *network* programming.[14] Since news is not all political and since public affairs include more than electoral issues, the actual political/electoral content of broadcasting is probably even lower. The "public issue" programming requirement is quite general, so that it is difficult to find broadcaster performance lacking under the requirement except in cases of clear irresponsibility. Public affairs programming deficiencies alone have never resulted in the loss of a license.

The concept of *equal time* applies specifically to the use of broadcasting by candidates for political office. In congressional debate on the first comprehensive radio law, it was pointed out that:

> The broadcasting field holds untold potentialities in a political . . . way; its future use in this respect will undoubtedly be extensive and effective. There is nothing . . . to prevent a broadcasting station from permitting one party or one candidate . . . to employ its service and refusing to accord the same right to the opposing side.[15]

Accordingly, Congress therefore gave candidates for public office the right of access to broadcast time on a station if another candidate for the same office is given or sold time on the station. Section 315 of the Communications Act, often referred to as the "equal time" provision, states that "if any licensee shall permit any person who is a legally qualified candidate for any public office to use a broadcasting station, he shall afford equal opportunities to all other such candidates for that office in the use of such broadcasting station." [16] The provision does not require that the broadcast time made available to a candidate be absolutely equal in either length or scheduling to that of his opponent, but it requires that it should be closely equivalent, with the format under the candidate's control.[17]

In 1959, the FCC held that under the equal time provision, Lar "America First" Daly, a minor mayoral candidate in Chicago, was entitled to broadcast time to balance a brief film clip on a television newscast showing Mayor Richard J. Daley, who was a candidate for reelection, welcoming a foreign visitor. Broadcasters and congressmen interpreted this decision to mean that if elected officials received even brief news coverage, time must be made available to all candidates opposing them for reelection. This, they said, would effectively bar news of public figures from the air, at least during campaign periods. As a result, Congress amended the law to exempt from the equal time requirement appearances on bona fide newscasts, news interviews, news documentaries (if the candidate's appearance was incidental to the subject), and on-the-spot coverage of actual news events.[18] This amendment in effect exempts from the equal-time provision programs in which format, content, and scheduling are controlled by the broadcaster rather than the candidate.[19]

The equal time provision applies only to individuals, not to issues or institutions. The right to equal time can be exercised only by a candidate, not by his supporters or his party.[20] The provision gives access to a political party or to Congress only to the extent that the individual candidate represents them.

The right to equal time is set in motion by the appearance of a candidate on a nonexempt program, whether or not the content of the appearance is political. The "nonpolitical" appearance of a president who has announced his candidacy for reelection may give his opponents the right to broadcast time. In 1964 CBS asked the FCC whether the broadcast of President Johnson's news conferences would give his opponent, Barry Goldwater, a right to equivalent broadcast time; the commission ruled that it would because both men were nominated candidates for the presidency and because the news conferences, largely controlled in scheduling and format by the president, were not exempt as news events.[21] The FCC also has held that a president-candidate's appearance on a televised "kick-off" for the United Fund and Community Chest would entitle opposing candidates to "equal opportunities," despite the apparently non-partisan nature of the appearance.[22]

When a president talks and acts like a candidate for reelection but has not announced his candidacy, no equal time obligation is created. This freedom from challenge is an enormous advantage. A president may begin running for reelection immediately after he is first elected; many of his appearances may contain partisan commentary and all his appearances, taken together, can create an image designed to ensure his reelection— but so long as he is not an official candidate, his opposition has no way to counter him. Even as an election approaches and presidential opponents announce their candidacies, a president who remains an unannounced candidate can engage in politicking on television without fear that he is creating a right of access for his opposition. Moreover, the president who announces merely that he is a candidate for *his party's nomination* for the presidency does not invite challenge, since the law creates equality only between candidates for exactly the same position. It does not give a candidate for the *opposition party's nomination* the right to equal time.

Even as skilled and astute a television campaigner as President Nixon did not realize fully the extent of his advantage. Early in 1972, he was interviewed by correspondent Dan Rather in prime time on the CBS television network. By then George McGovern had been a candidate for the Democratic 1972 presidential nomination for many months; Hubert Humphrey, Edmund Muskie, and George Wallace all were obvious candidates for the same nomination. During the course of the interview, the president, recognizing the advantage of his appearance politically, observed that the Democrats probably would seek "equal time." The president's assumption was reasonable but not legally sound because his "opponents" were then candidates only for the presidential nomination of a different party and, under the equal time law, had no right to counter the president's appearance.

A president maintains his political edge even after he has been formally nominated by his party for reelection since not all his television appearances will bring his opponents equal time. Sometimes not even his most important appearances will. On October 31, 1956, less than a week before the national election, President Eisenhower, the Republican candidate running for reelection, addressed the nation for fifteen minutes on the Suez crisis. The Democratic candidate, Adlai Stevenson, asked the networks for equal time. His request denied, he appealed to the FCC. The FCC decided against ruling, saying there was not time enough to deal with such a complex matter. But rather than risk violating the equal time law, the networks gave time to Stevenson and four minor party candidates. Stevenson spoke on November 1 on all networks. On Monday, November 5, the day before the election, the FCC reversed itself and ruled that Eisenhower's address did not create an equal time responsibility, stating, "we do not believe that when Congress enacted Section 315 it intended to grant equal time to all Presidential candidates when the President uses the air lanes in reporting to the Nation on an international crisis." [23] The networks were in a dilemma, and saw no way out except to achieve balance by offering Eisenhower time to reply to Stevenson. The problem was resolved when Eisenhower's campaign managers declined the offer.

Less than two weeks before the 1964 presidential election, President Johnson, who was then running for reelection, preempted prime-time network television to report to the nation on a series of important international events—the fall of Khrushchev, explosion of a nuclear bomb by mainland China, and the fall of the Labour government in England. (His speech had the effect of drawing attention away from an incident involving a member of his staff that might have been blown up to damage his campaign.) Immediately Senator Goldwater, the Republican candidate, and Louis Jaeckel, American Party candidate, requested "equal time" from the networks. When they were denied, they appealed to the FCC. Citing the law's exemptions for bona fide news events and the 1956 Eisenhower case, the FCC held that the president's speech was exempt from the equal time requirement.[24] Yet in such major addresses delivered at the very height of the campaign, a president has complete control over whether, when, and for how long he appears on television; he reaches a "captive" audience on all three networks simultaneously; and he is subject to no questioning or rebuttal. On the basis of the decisions in the Eisenhower and Johnson cases, he can do all this for free, without "equal opportunities" for his political opponents.

Both the concept of equal time and the way in which it is implemented have an inhibiting effect on balanced political broadcasting between the presidential candidates of the two major political parties. The networks grant the requests of a president who also is a candidate for reelection but they are understandably reluctant to make time available to his principal opponent because to do so whould invite sudden appearances by candidates of minor parties. Television and radio licensees might have been more willing to make time available for Adlai Stevenson in 1956 or Barry Goldwater in 1960 had the equal time provision not required equal access to minor party candidates however insignificant they may be in the nation at large. Minor parties have had a legitimate and frequently significant place in the nation's political life but the notion that their presidential candidates merit the same treatment as the candidates of the major parties has restricted political debate on television.

In 1972, for example, the FCC ruled that an appearance on

a Walt Disney television show entitled "The Mouse Factory" by comedian Pat Paulsen, then a candidate in the New Hampshire Republican primary, would entitle other candidates (President Nixon and Congressmen Ashbrook and McCloskey) for the nomination to equal time. Two candidates also requested and received equal time when Paulsen appeared for twenty seconds in the rerun of an old movie on the NBC network. The imposition of such demands on broadcasters in behalf of equal time is hardly conducive to getting them to volunteer air time to a major opposition party during a presidential election campaign.[25]

Clearly, the equal time law does not meet the challenge posed by presidential television. A president may use television for political objectives throughout his incumbency, but the law provides his opposition with television opportunities in the fourth year of his term and then only late in the election campaign. Major presidential addresses, even those delivered but days before an election, may go unanswered under the law. And finally the decision to treat candidates of minor parties the same way as the candidates of major national parties has limited coverage of all candidates, except of course the president.

The concept of *fairness* in broadcasting regulation applies not to candidates or parties but to issues. The "fairness doctrine" was developed by the FCC as an administrative interpretation of the Communications Act; it is not, as equal time is, set forth in detail in the law itself. Briefly stated, fairness calls for a balanced presentation of different points of view, so that "when a broadcast station presents one side of a controversial issue of public importance, the Commission's fairness doctrine requires that reasonable opportunity be afforded for the presentation of contrasting views." [26] To former FCC Chairman E. William Henry, "It is as simple as that. All the rest is commentary." [27]

While not as precise as the "equal time" provisions, the fairness doctrine obligates the licensee, under the statutory "public interest" standard, to make reasonable judgments in good faith as to whether both sides of "controversial issues of public importance" have been fairly presented in the course of his overall programming. The objective is not per-program or per-week equality, but simply a general balance over time between major positions on important and controversial issues. Broadcasters are obligated to take positive steps to encourage the presentation of these contrasting views over their facilities, including presenting some views free if commercial sponsors cannot be found.[28] The FCC has held matters as varied as fluoridation, nutrition, integration, pay-TV, private pilots, and cigarette smoking to be both controversial and of public importance; it also has decided that religion and army recruiting are noncontroversial issues.

In aiming for fairness, the FCC has determined that broadcast time provided for presentation of views on controversial issues need not be equal or even roughly approximate.[29] But its decisions have suggested that a marked difference in format, allowing one position to be presented through a speech while confining the other to an interview, might not be satisfactory.[30] The FCC also has ruled it would be "patently unreasonable" for a licensee to present one side in prime evening time and the other in the daytime consistently.[31] Quantity of time, too, can affect fairness balance. When one side of an issue—cigarette ads, for example—is presented repetitively, the other side— anti-cigarette spots—has been held entitled to similar, if not equal, repetition. Although repetition may not convey any new information, it may well increase the effectiveness of an advocate's message.[32]

The emphasis of the fairness doctrine rests squarely on issues, and little attention has been accorded the individual or group presenting them. As the doctrine has evolved, no specific person or group is entitled to present views on radio or television because of the fairness doctrine except for three special exceptions:

1. Individuals or groups personally attacked in a discussion of controversial issues of public importance. In such cases, the broadcaster must offer the individuals or groups "a reasonable opportunity to respond." [33]
2. Candidates who have been editorialized against by a broadcast station or whose political opposition has been endorsed by a station. In these cases, the broadcaster must make "an offer of a reasonable opportunity for a candidate or a spokesman of the candidate to respond." [34]
3. Political parties during election campaigns, which is the subject of the FCC's special "political party doctrine."

In each of the three cases, it is assumed that the affected individual or group is so clearly the appropriate respondent that no room is left for a choice of spokesman.

The FCC views its role in enforcing fairness doctrine obligations as "not to substitute its judgment for that of the licensee . . . , but rather to determine whether the licensee can be said to have acted reasonably and in good faith." [35] In carrying out its responsibility, it does not monitor stations for adherence to the fairness doctrine but depends upon complaints from listeners. Because fairness is difficult to determine, the complaining individual or group bears the burden of proving its complaint. The procedure itself often is protracted anyway; even if the aggrieved party succeeds in proving his case, he may not be able to make a timely response. A substantial degree of discretion has to be left to the broadcaster, who selects spokesmen for the various positions on controversial issues and allocates the time for their presentation. Generally, to gain access to radio or television under the fairness doctrine, one must be chosen by a broadcaster as an appropriate spokesman for a point of view that the broadcaster believes to be controversial, of public importance, and not adequately presented in other programming.

Much of the controversy involving fairness concerns attempts by opposition parties or candidates to counter the presentations made by incumbents. Presidential television, of course, is at the heart of the problem. According to the FCC, "there is no question but that fairness doctrine is applicable to Presidential addresses on controversial issues of public importance," [36] but it has required only that stations that have carried presidential addresses also present, at some time during the course of their programming, viewpoints opposing those of the president on domestic or international issues. These views could be presented by station commentators, in news specials, by the appearance of local groups or in other ways, none of which necessarily includes an appearance by a member of the opposition party or of Congress in a prime-time, uninterrupted broadcast.

The FCC's application of the doctrine of fairness to the president's use of television was a gradual development. In 1950, CBS radio stations in New York State broadcast a "report to the People of New York" by Governor Thomas E. Dewey, a Republican. The New York Democratic State Committee complained to CBS that the Dewey broadcast was controversial, politically motivated, and political in content. It asked that it be balanced by a Democratic presentation. CBS argued that the governor's address was simply a report to his constituents and regarded it as neither "controversial" nor political. The FCC upheld CBS.[37] But its decision recognized that political incumbents may be inviting controversy in their broadcasts:

> On the other hand, it is apparent that so-called reports to the people may constitute attacks on the opposite political party or may be a discussion of a public controversial issue. . . . [It] is clear that the characterization of a particular program as a non-political address or . . . as a report to the people does not necessarily establish such a program as non-controversial in nature so as to avoid the requirement of affording time for the expression of opposing views.[38]

Even in such a case, the opposing views would not necessarily have to be presented by the opposition party or its spokesmen.

Some years later, the FCC, responding to another complaint that a program featuring local officials presented only one side of a controversial issue, affirmed that "the fact that the proponents of one particular position on . . . an issue are elected officials does not in any way . . . remove the applicability of our fair presentation policy." [39] Again, the FCC determined that an address by California's Governor Reagan on taxes, college tuition, and legislative proposals could not be immune from fairness obligations. [40] But the major opposition party spokesman was given no special status.

The first attempt to apply the fairness doctrine to a presidential appearance was made shortly before the 1960 election. The retiring president, Eisenhower, who was not a candidate for reelection, delivered an address in San Francisco. The California Democratic State Central Committee labeled the speech partisan and political and asked the San Francisco stations that had carried it to provide comparable time. The stations denied this request, arguing, in the FCC's words, that:

> The Office of the Presidency of the United States is of such high dignity that [a station] must accept the assurance by the White House in each case whether the President's appearance is or is not non-political and . . . it is entirely inappropriate to provide time for reply to a Presidential appearance which he designates as non-political. . . . [41]

The FCC upheld the broadcasters in deciding that the "noncontroversial" label on the Eisenhower speech was not unreasonable. It considered the address only in terms of its explicit content, without reference to its political implications so close to an election. The importance of its decision was that it extended to the presidency the principle that the appearance of an elected official must be "considered in the light of whether it involves a discussion of controversial issues of public importance. If it does, then the station has an obligation to afford reasonable opportunity for the presentation of opposing views."

In October of 1964, when President Johnson delivered his address on foreign affairs, the Republican National Committee requested comparable television time for Senator Goldwater under both the equal time and fairness doctrines. The networks refused, arguing that Goldwater's views on the subjects covered by Johnson had been covered adequately in regular news and public affairs programs. The RNC complained to the FCC. As it had in 1960, the FCC held that although the fairness doctrine applied to a president's address, the networks had already fulfilled their fairness obligation by presenting views similar to those of Senator Goldwater.[42]

Late in 1967, President Johnson went on all three networks for a "conversation" on Vietnam. Senator Eugene McCarthy, running for the 1968 Democratic presidential nomination, asked to respond. In rejecting his complaint, the FCC noted that the Vietnam issue had been thoroughly treated by the networks. CBS, for example, had previously presented McCarthy himself as a guest on a network interview program and had also broadcast on "Face the Nation" interviews with Senator Mark Hatfield, Senator Robert F. Kennedy, Governor George Romney, Senator Stuart Symington, Mayor John Lindsay, and Dr. Benjamin Spock, all of whom, in varying degrees, took exception to the administration's Vietnam policy. Moreover, CBS's regular news broadcasts had included extensive coverage of the views of those opposed to the administration's policy on Vietnam.

But in disposing of the McCarthy complaint, the FCC again applied the fairness test only to the issue of Vietnam itself, not to the political implications of presidential television. Senator McCarthy had sought television parity with the president not only because he had differing views on the war but also because he wanted to present his image and personality, as the president had, to the electorate. For the same reasons, the Democrats had vainly sought television time to respond to Eisenhower in 1960 and the Republicans had vainly tried to respond to Johnson in 1964.

In recent years, groups seeking to respond to television commercials have forced some recognition from the FCC and the courts that important controversial issues may be raised implicitly in a television presentation—racial issues in charity appeals, for example, ecology issues in an oil company corporate "image" ad.[43] But the FCC ignored the issues implicit in presidential television until 1970.

In 1970, in response to the fairness complaints of senators, businessmen, professors, and students about President Nixon's use of television, the FCC based its decision on its prior fairness doctrine decisions. It analyzed overall network programming on Vietnam and determined that the programming— news, interviews, panel shows, and documentaries—had been balanced between pro- and anti-administration viewpoints, *except* for many presidential addresses. Since all other programming had been balanced, the uninterrupted, prime-time addresses had definitely tipped the scales in favor of the president's position.[44] In these circumstances, said the FCC, the networks must select a spokesman to present the opposing viewpoint in one more uninterrupted program.

Thus, for the first time ever, the FCC ordered free television time for a response to a presidential appearance. But the FCC addressed only the specific substantive issue and left the choice of a spokesman to the networks. It gave neither the Committee for Fair Broadcasting nor the senators nor the businessmen a right to broadcast time. In fact, the FCC specifically rejected the suggestion that the senators' positions as senators should give them a special claim to access. It also disavowed any intention to create a doctrine requiring regular responses to presidential television or equality in format.[45] When the press interpreted this decision as a grant of equal time for the presidential opposition, FCC Chairman Dean Burch issued a separate statement: "We have expressly rejected any principle embodying right of reply or rebuttal to the President." [46]

The FCC continues to maintain that no one—including the opposition political party or members of Congress—has the right to be the spokesman for a point of view different from the president's. Even when it finds an imbalance in the presentation of views, the commission will "of course leave entirely to the judgment of the networks the selection of the appropriate spokesman" for the other side.[47] Moreover, it is still far from conceding that a presidential appearance, because of its impact on the roles of the opposition party and Congress, can be a fairness issue itself.

Evolving from the fairness doctrine and the equal time law, the FCC's *political party doctrine* requires that if one of the major political parties is either given or sold broadcast time to discuss candidate or election issues, the other major party must also be given or allowed to purchase time. This administrative doctrine is another attempt to ensure balance. It also is intended to close a loophole in the equal time law, one that might enable a party spokesman to use television time to promote a candidate without creating an "equal time" right for the opposition candidate. It has developed from earlier FCC "fairness" rulings that broadcasters should make reasonable efforts to achieve equality in the treatment of political parties—they must, for example, broadcast the national convention of both major political parties if they broadcast the convention of either; [48] they must broadcast announcements soliciting party campaign funds in a roughly equivalent manner.[49] But the political party doctrine represents an exceptional application of fairness because it designates a spokesman and recognizes the political importance of particular television appearances regardless of the substantive issues discussed.

The FCC created the political party doctrine in 1970 in response to a series of hypothetical questions posed by Nicholas Zapple, staff counsel to the Senate Commerce Committee. The FCC told Zapple that "where a spokesman for, or supporter of Candidate A buys time and broadcasts a discussion of the candidates or the campaign issues . . . , spokesmen for or supporters of opposing Candidate B are not only appropriate, but the logical spokesmen for presenting contrasting views." [50] In most cases, the FCC went on, "it would not be reasonable" for a licensee to refuse to sell comparable time to the Democratic party, for example, when a Republican party spokesman has purchased or been given time to discuss candidates or election issues. This decision recognized, if only to a limited extent, that when partisan politics are involved, the appropriate respondent to one party's spokesman is the other party's spokesman.

But in applying its political party doctrine, the FCC has exempted presidential television. In one of its first attempts to define the doctrine's scope, the FCC acknowledged that a presidential appearance might well constitute an endorsement of the president's party because his role as commander-in-chief could not be separated from his role as party leader. It also recognized that if the president was not an announced candidate for reelection, or if his appearance was considered a news event, his appearance did not create an "equal time" right for the opposition party candidate. In spite of all this, however, the FCC concluded that though unfairness might result, the president must be treated as a national leader who was above partisan politics and to whom the political party doctrine would not apply. As the FCC concluded, "thus, when the President delivers a veto message or informs the nation concerning his decision on Cambodia, he is not making an appearance within the 'political' party doctrine." [51]

More recently the FCC has held that the doctrine is to be interpreted as applying only to appearances of supporters of candidates,[52] not to candidates themselves. Accordingly, when a president running for reelection goes on television, if the "equal time" law does not require an opportunity for the opposition to respond, neither will the political party doctrine.

Because it is relatively new, the political party doctrine has not yet been fully developed. Its interpretations to date, however, seem unlikely to provide significant broadcast access for party or congressional opponents of the president. Indeed, thus far, its practical effect actually has limited opposition television access. When CBS initiated its "Loyal Opposition" series in 1970 to provide the opposition party with increased television exposure, the president's party invoked the doctrine to demand time to respond—and the FCC granted it. Although the FCC decision subsequently was reversed by the courts because it had failed to provide a clear rationale for its ruling, the controversy caused CBS to discontinue the "Loyal Opposition" series. It was three years before the network tried again, this time with a policy of giving time to various spokesmen of its choosing, not necessarily representatives of the opposition party or Congress, to respond to presidential addresses.

In short, the regulatory law and doctrines that have evolved over the years do not meet the problems created by presidential television. Although the FCC maintains that political programming is essential to broadcast operation in the public interest, this requirement does not appear to have increased the amount of such programming. To be sure, formally announced candidates whose opponents have appeared on television have the right to equal time—except when the opponent is the president and his appearance deals with important national issues. If the president has not announced his candidacy for reelection, his opposition cannot claim equal time even though his real campaign may have gone on for four years. A major political party has a right to buy time if the other major party buys or is given time—but, again, the president, though in fact the preeminent leader of his party, is not considered a party member for this purpose. The fairness doctrine also recognizes that repetition of a message may increase its effectiveness and that an automobile commercial can implicitly raise the issue of pollution, but it does not recognize that a presidential address, or frequent prime-time presidential television appearances, can by implication convey a political message. None of this legal machinery makes broadcast time available to party and congressional opposition to balance the president's automatic access to the television audience.

CHAPTER 4

CONGRESS, COURT, AND CAMERA

THE CONSTITUTION OF THE UNITED STATES speaks of checks and balances, of the equality among the three branches of government; but it provides no guidance for preserving that balance in the electronic age. Many serious students of government believe that presidential television threatens to tilt the constitutional balance of powers in favor of the president. No legal doctrine gives the legislative or judicial branches the right to appear on television to balance a president's presentation or to initiate debate on presidential policy. Moreover, those two branches have seldom if ever systematically sought television access. Indeed, they have tended to avoid it.

During the administrations of President Johnson and President Nixon, congressional critics of presidential policy complained that the president was usurping congressional power and upsetting the constitutional balance. Their complaints began over the president's war powers. Later they broadened to challenge his right to refuse to spend money the Congress had appropriated. By 1973, the question had burgeoned into a great debate. In all this, television played no inconsiderable role.

THE SUPREME COURT

Like the president, the members of the Supreme Court have always been treated with deference; the president because he is the chief of state, the justices because they are, in theory, above politics. While presidents have used their position to increase their access to the broadcast media, the Court has used its position to avoid it. The Supreme Court has shunned television and has done little to improve its coverage by journalists. While the president's prestige has grown, the Court's ability to counter him has diminished.

In recent years, controversy over the Court has grown. President Nixon's criticism of Supreme Court decisions has enmeshed the Court in partisan politics. His criticism has gone unanswered, and the Court avoids publicity. The Senate has refused to confirm two of his Supreme Court nominees, further involving the Court in partisan strife. An attempt has been made in the House to impeach one incumbent justice—more politics. Court decisions have begun to reverse the trend of the Warren Court. And because the Court stands aloof, the entire controversy has been murky, the issues shrouded in darkness for all but experts.

The Court has always prohibited live broadcasting from anywhere within its tabernacle, even from telephone booths. Television news organizations rarely cover the Court at all. Carl Stern, NBC's Court correspondent, has estimated that he reports on the Court only about six times a year.[1] Former Chief Justice Earl Warren granted his first national television interview in 1972, three years after he had left the Court.

Broadcasting equipment has traditionally been barred from all courtrooms. When radio was still new in the 1930s, microphones were allowed in court at the judge's discretion. But after the sensational trial of Bruno Hauptmann in the Charles Lindbergh kidnapping case, which was broadcast in full, the American Bar Association adopted a prohibition against cameras and microphones in court. The association later extended the prohibition to television. Though the ABA action is not the law of the land, the Federal Rules of Criminal Procedure, which have the effect of law, prohibit broadcasting and photography in criminal courtrooms.[2] And in 1964, the Supreme Court upheld the exclusion of broadcasting from courtrooms when it upset the conviction of a Texas financier, Billy Sol Estes, on the ground that television cameras in the courtroom where he was tried had deprived him of a fair trial.[3] The majority opinion held that televised criminal trials were inherently unfair, depriving defendants of the due process of law guaranteed by the Fourteenth Amendment. The opinion reasoned that televising criminal trials could make jurors realize that they were dealing with a *cause célèbre,* could distract them, could affect the behavior of witnesses—demoralizing or embarrassing them or making them "cocky"—could oblige the trial judge to rule again and again on questions of the propriety of televising various parts of the trial. And it could harm the defendant. "Its [television's] presence is a form of mental—if not physical—harassment resembling a police line-up or the third degree," the Court declared.[4]

The printed press reports Court decisions fully—but with difficulty. The Court issues no press releases. Until recently it held no press conferences or briefings. Its basement press room is so small that some reporters must stand as they read the day's decisions. On days when the Court renders decisions by oral delivery newsmen wait in the basement press room. As the reading begins, a signal is given to the Court's press officer, who then releases copies of the day's opinions and distributes them. Reporters are sometimes obliged to deal—under deadline pressure—with several complex and difficult opinions at one time.

The Court's relations with the press have never been entirely smooth. Before the Civil War, an associate justice released a dissenting opinion in the famous Dred Scott case [5] upholding the fugitive slave law even before Chief Justice Roger B. Taney had finished writing his majority opinion.[6] Incensed, Taney ordered the clerk of the Court not to release its opinions until they appeared in the official compilation of Court decisions, and this order remained in force until the twentieth century.

The Court did not begin giving reporters full texts of opinions immediately after oral delivery until after a journalistic mishap. In a 1920 decision, the Court held that corporate stock dividends were not taxable as ordinary income.[7] The justices read their opinions in an almost inaudible mumble. Dow-Jones misunderstood and reported the opposite result. Stock prices fell until the error was corrected.[8]

The current policy of releasing decisions to the press as soon as the justices begin to read them followed another press bungle. An Associated Press reporter, after hearing just a few minutes of a lengthy and complex opinion on Congress's power to invalidate "gold clauses" in private contracts, chose and filed precisely the wrong paragraph from among the one hundred leads he had prewritten for the occasion. Thereafter, the Court began releasing opinions as they were read orally.

When the Court handed down its decision in *Engel* v. *Vitale* [9] declaring unconstitutional the compulsory recitation of daily prayers in New York State schools, the Court came under fire from the public, and Court correspondents came under fire from the legal profession. The press, its critics claimed, was more interested in arousing public outrage than in making the precise holding of the Court clear. The decision did not ban religious observance from public life, nor did it strike down the concept of God, press critics complained, but the headlines and news stories left those impressions. As a result of this controversy, the Association of American Law Schools established a program to provide newsmen with brief explanations of cases pending before the court. Unfortunately, this practice was discontinued in 1972, and newsmen are again left to struggle alone and unaided.

After the school prayer controversy, Chief Justice Warren promised to end the practice of releasing all Court decisions on Mondays. Spreading the decisions through the week would give reporters more time to write their stories, increasing the probability of accuracy. Chief Justice Warren Burger made good Warren's promise in 1970.[10]

The Court moves slowly in increasing its exposure to the press. In 1968, Justice Black granted an interview to two CBS television reporters. In 1971, after the Court decision in the case of Muhammad Ali, the former boxing champion, Justice Thurgood Marshall sent a note to reporters in the Court's press room explaining that he had not voted on the decision because he had been the government's chief prosecutor at the time of Ali's indictment, thus heading off speculation that he had abstained because of his and Ali's color. Chief Justice Burger, shortly after he took office, asked reporters to recommend changes in Court procedures that would make their job easier and promote reliable reporting. A group of reporters responded with several proposals, including suggestions that the Court provide a brief summary of each opinion and lock up reporters with copies of decisions in advance of the Court's announcement.[11]

In 1970, Chief Justice Burger delivered a "State of the Judiciary" report at the annual meeting of the American Bar Association and allowed television to broadcast it, although he has refused to permit television coverage of other speeches. He has, however, held a "background briefing" for newspaper correspondents on the controversial school busing case and other issues, and once he granted an exclusive on-the-record interview with *U.S. News and World Report*.[12] In order to accommodate reporters, he arranged that the daily list of Court orders be released in advance to the press, that headnotes (summaries of the decisions on the legal points involved in the case) accompany Court opinions, that opinions be spread out through the week, and that delivery of newsworthy opinions be scheduled to allow reporters time to cover oral arguments.[13]

The Court has traditionally avoided publicity in order to protect itself from political pressures. During the constitutional debates, Alexander Hamilton argued that only a judiciary removed from the other affairs of government could guard against demagogues and schemers and the "effect of occasional ill humors in the society." [14] As Alexander Bickel, a Yale law professor, has written, "justices have their being near the political marketplace. . . . But the system embodies elaborate mechanisms for insulation." [15] These mechanisms include the Court's ability to avoid decisions on controversial cases by refusing to hear them or deciding the cases on narrow, legalistic grounds; the removal of the Court from the public eye; and the appointment of justices for life, subject only to "good behavior," eliminating their need to cultivate public opinion for reappointment.

The Court does not wish to comment on the cases it decides because it is the written opinions of the Court which guide the public and the lower courts. The precise language of the opinion itself makes law. To add to it would change it. Former Chief Justice Warren has observed that beyond their formal written opinions, the justices cannot explain their actions: "You can't temper the thing in any way . . . and that's one reason why the courts are traduced so much in this country. . . . They have no way of talking back, where a man who's in politics can fight as hard as he wants to do it." [16] In addition, judges always have hesitated to comment on issues they may have to face in court.

Ever since the days of George Washington, the Supreme Court has refused to comment upon issues not presented as concrete cases before the bar. Even the president cannot receive general legal advice from the Court because of this rule against advisory opinions. Few would attack this tradition.

For all these reasons, it appears, the Supreme Court has good cause to remain as aloof as possible from the maelstrom of national television and partisan politics. And yet this leaves unanswered: What of public opinion?

True, Supreme Court justices do not have to seek public favor and run for reelection. Nonetheless, in the long run, the Court needs to have its decisions supported by public opinion. For the constitutional basis of the Court's power is far more fragile than the president's or Congress's. The framers of the Constitution explicitly gave the Congress control over money. They explicitly made the president commander-in-chief of the military. But they gave the Supreme Court and its subordinate courts only the power to decide legal cases arising under the Constitution, federal laws and treaties, and disputes between citizens of different states. In 1803, Chief Justice John Marshall, in *Marbury* v. *Madison,*[17] laid out the theory of judicial review. Under this doctrine, if the Court were given a law to apply that did not square with the Constitution as the justices read it, the Court would refuse to apply the law. Marshall thus ascribed to the Court the power to overrule acts of Congress and the president.

But this power is severely limited. No one ever stated the limitation more bluntly than President Andrew Jackson when he refused to act on a Supreme Court finding that a Georgia law restricting Cherokee Indian rights was unconstitutional. "John Marshall has made his decision," Jackson said; "now let him enforce it." [18] The Court generally depends on the president for enforcement of its decisions, not only by direct executive action—orders to the Department of Justice or even the

National Guard—but also by presidential leadership of public opinion. But with public support behind him, the president may seriously impede, by his statements and actions, the practical effectiveness of a Court decision. Public opinion, therefore, can have considerable influence on the checking and balancing done by the Court.

Popular opinion helps to set the frontiers of judicial decision-making. Supreme Court decisions that provoke widespread popular antipathy will often come back to harass the justices. In the early nineteenth century, Alexis de Tocqueville wrote, "Their power is enormous, but it is clothed in the authority of public opinion. They are the all-powerful guardians of a people which respects law; but they would be impotent against popular neglect or popular contempt." [19] Of course, the Court has never made a practice of shaping its decisions in accordance with majority whim. But public opinion does mark off a line beyond which the Court steps only at great danger to itself.

The Court has more than once stepped beyond this line and defied the president. As Justice Robert Jackson wrote, "It has been in collision with the most dynamic and popular Presidents in our history." [20] Jefferson tried to have Justice Salmon Chase impeached in 1804. Jefferson lost. Franklin Roosevelt tried to reorganize the Court to his own liking. Roosevelt lost. Harry Truman learned his lesson, and acquiesced in the Court's decision that he could not constitutionally nationalize the steel industry to prevent a shutdown. And most presidents have been careful not to confront the Supreme Court head-on.

If the president should ever go on television or radio to campaign directly against the Court, it seems almost certain that the networks would grant a request from the Supreme Court for rebuttal time; the news value alone would be immense. But presidential leverage over the judiciary need not depend on the president's ability to attack the Court outright on television. A president can damage a silent Court simply by remaining silent himself.

On the morning of September 4, 1956, school children all over the United States prepared for their first day of classes. Nine black children in Little Rock, Arkansas, had more to fear than other children. They aimed to integrate the all-white Central High School that morning. Two hundred fifty National Guardsmen planted firmly around the school aimed to stop them. Governor Orval Faubus had told his state that he would not allow integration to proceed despite the Supreme Court ruling in *Brown* v. *Board of Education* [21] calling for school desegregation "with all deliberate speed." Faubus's defiance formed but a part of a movement throughout the South to nullify the *Brown* decision.

President Eisenhower watched the battle develop between the federal judiciary and the southern states'-rights advocates. But he remained mute. When several congressmen protested that he was not performing his duty to enforce the Court's edict, Eisenhower replied, through his special counsel, "The President would not make any assumption that the judicial branch of the Government is incapable of implementing the Supreme Court's decision." [22] Beneath the diplomatic language lurked Jackson's ultimatum: they made the law; let them enforce it.

Eisenhower's silence gave the Court's opponents strength enough to force a showdown at Little Rock. Faubus's plan ultimately failed, less because he was defying the supreme law of the land than because the situation in Little Rock got out of hand; violence broke out quickly, and the television cameras recorded it all for the appalled American people. Faubus had overplayed his hand. On September 24, Eisenhower finally acted, ordering federal troops into Little Rock, not to integrate the schools but to prevent the breakdown of local law enforcement. Eisenhower's silence, regardless of his intent, impeded the orderly enforcement of the Supreme Court's holding.

President Nixon, too, lessened the ability of a silent Court to affect national policy. More than any president since Franklin Roosevelt, Nixon has publicized his discontent with the Supreme Court. During his 1968 campaign he charged the Court with "giving the green light" to criminals by liberalizing criminal procedural safeguards for defendants.[23] He has often indicated disagreement with the Court's ruling that the busing of students to achieve school integration is not improper. That decision has aroused the ire of busing's foes, many of whom are under the mistaken impression that it requires busing. The president has done little to promote public acceptance of the ruling.

Both Eisenhower's response to the *Brown* decision and Nixon's response to busing showed the power of the executive branch. The president could take action or refrain from action to enforce the decision. He could speak or fail to speak to the people through the media. The Court has relied on the president to support its decision. Without this support, Court decisions lose some of their effectiveness and the Court loses some of its prestige.

Were the Court to request television time to defend its positions against presidential criticism, it is easy to conjure up innumerable confrontations—on the Court's overturn of FDR's AAA and NRA, on the steel seizure, on school desegregation in all its aspects including busing, on Court appointees, on the decisions of the Warren Court on the procedural rights of defendants in criminal trials, such as the Miranda case, which required the police to warn criminal suspects that they have the right to remain silent and to have an attorney present during police questioning—indeed, on the whole range of "law and order" issues.

As things stand now, such televised confrontations would appear more damaging to the country than enlightening. True, they would give the Court opportunity to disseminate and defend its decisions. They would enable the Court to educate the public about its functions. And television broadcasts of actual Supreme Court proceedings might clarify issues before the

Court and help the public understand them. But, on the other hand, such confrontations would also inflame controversy; they would further divide the country; they would diminish the Court's prestige and throw the Court, that aloof final arbiter, into the whirlpool of controversial political television.

Because television conveys individual images so well, the entry of the Court into television could focus public attention on the personalities of justices, not on their decisions. The medium of the law is written language. Television "explanations" of decisions by the Court would make it extremely difficult to determine the precise holding of the decisions—the "explanations" might be taken as part of the decisions themselves. The Supreme Court is not like the Congress. It is not like the opposition party. It is not like the presidency. Its members do not have to run for reelection. They represent the ultimate authority. They are the living symbol of a government of laws, not men, and thus they are the rock-bottom foundation of the democratic system in the United States. To put them into confrontation, television would risk destroying their entire position.

Conceivably, a time may come when the justices will decide that they wish to go before the country to explain a decision or defend a position against presidential attack. They should, and in practice would, have the right to make such a defense. But until that time comes, it seems unwise to thrust TV access upon them. They should reserve to themselves the right to decide their own course, just as they reserve the right to decide which cases to review.

At the same time, however, it is urged that the press and the bar devote greater attention to how Court decisions are reported. The schools of journalism, in cooperation with the law schools, should offer specialized training to equip newsmen with the legal background they need to cover the Court. Editors should encourage specialization in Court coverage. The networks and the educational broadcasters could better inform the public by presenting documentary or even dramatized backgrounds of important decisions. Lawyers should help broadcasters understand and present Supreme Court cases.

Both the public and the Court would benefit. Public understanding would strengthen the Court against such political sloganeering as "impeach Earl Warren," "strict constructionists," "forced busing," and "unconstitutional prayers." Adequate reporting of the Court would tend to balance presidential criticism of it and perhaps make it unnecessary for the Court to be drawn into an arena foreign to its traditions.

CONGRESS

The case of the Congress is far different. The Supreme Court justices have not sought access to television to balance the president. But senators and representatives have. The Court's immense prestige and nonpartisan nature have helped it withstand presidential attack. Congress has no comparable prestige and is intensely partisan. The president's access to television has not yet destroyed the Court's ability to balance him. But it may well have weakened that of the Congress. In recent years numerous suggestions have been made that the Congress needs access to balance presidential television; and it is to this question that we now turn.

In dividing the powers of government, the framers of the Constitution were particularly concerned about what they saw as a natural tendency of legislative authority to "intrude upon the rights, and to absorb the powers of the other departments." [24] Congress was considered naturally more powerful than the president largely because legislators had greater access to the people:

> The members of the executive . . . are few in number, and can be personally known to a small part only of the people. . . .

The members of the legislative department, on the other hand, are numerous. They are distributed and dwell among the people at large. . . . The nature of their public trust implies a personal influence among the people, and that they are more immediately the confidential guardians of the rights and liberties of the people. With these advantages it can hardly be supposed that the adverse party [the executive or judiciary] would have an equal chance for a favorable issue.[25]

The modern trend in American government, however, is toward an increasingly powerful president and an increasingly weak Congress. Presidential power has expanded because of the growth in national involvement in foreign affairs, because of the increasing role of the federal government in national life, especially in social services, and because television has given the president more access than Congress to the public.

When Franklin Roosevelt delivered a State of the Union address to the public on radio but had a stand-in read it to Congress, when John Kennedy went on national television to announce a blockade of Cuba, and when Richard Nixon vetoed an appropriations bill on the networks, each exercised power beyond Congress's ability to respond in kind. Although individual members of Congress may appear frequently on television in brief news clips or on Sunday interview programs, they have little or no access to prime television time under their own control.

Woodrow Wilson once remarked that the president "is the only national voice in affairs." [26] He alone represents the whole nation. The Congress, on the other hand, is composed of 435 representatives and 100 senators, each representing his own constituency, each holding his own views on nearly every issue. Television deals in images and can convey that of the one man in the White House more effectively than those of the 535 men and women in Congress. Similarly, because there is but one president, he can make news more easily than the average congressman. The press conference held by a senator probably will result in no live, prime-time coverage; a presidential press conference always will. The intricacies of congressional procedure, though of the utmost importance, may be uninteresting to watch and often incomprehensible to the public. Nor would it be easy to find a generally acceptable spokesman for the "view of Congress," to present on network television. Differences among the members of Congress often cross party and geographic lines; alignments shift issue by issue. As Frank Stanton, president of CBS, has said,

> And who would speak for an institution not conspicuous for its unanimity of expression even in the rare cases when there is near unanimity of view? Do the Speaker of the House and the President Pro Tempore of the Senate speak for all the members of their respective houses or only for the majority in each case? Would not the minority leaders and minority whips then want a voice—followed by the majority leaders and the majority whips? Would the chairmen of 59 joint, standing, select and special committees not insist on addressing themselves to the legislation referred to their committees—followed by the 59 ranking minority members of those committees? Would not then the sponsors of specific bills demand to be heard—followed by the opponents? In short, the only views of Congress are the views of its individual members—535 of them. Even presenting two at a time, it would take a broadcast every day including weekends for over eight months to present "the views of the Senate and the House of Representatives." [27]

Television has reversed the early concern that the president would be subordinate to the legislature because a single individual could not communicate as effectively with the populace as the multi-member Congress. The concern today must be directed to insuring that Congress can and will keep pace with presidential television. As FCC Commissioner Johnson has written, "if one branch of the government increasingly gains effective access to the media of communications, while the other branch is systematically excluded, then the power balance, presumably designed to safeguard our citizenry from the tyrannies and abuses of excessive power, will be upset." [28] Presidential dominance of prime-time network broadcasting can foreclose congressional competition. In the words of Democratic Senator Muskie, "this phenomenon . . . can virtually destroy the checks and balances so carefully established by our Constitution." [29] Republican Senator Charles Mathias, Jr., suggests it already is doing so: "Now, you can say—and you'd be right—that of course Congress can blow the whistle [on a presidential policy]. But with modern conditions, with the President able to appeal through the electronic media into every household, whereas the 535 members of Congress just appear as a babble of voices, it's very tough for Congress. . . ." [30]

Congress's only regular television access similar to the president's has been time provided by the networks for responses to the presidents' State of the Union addresses. Begun in the Eisenhower Administration, this once-a-year program has become traditional and usually presents opposition members of Congress. In 1970, at the invitation of the networks, Democrats in Congress presented an hour-long broadcast two weeks after the State of the Union message. The program, produced at a cost of $57,000, was broadcast on a Sunday afternoon simultaneously by two networks and later in the afternoon by the third network. The program showed about a dozen senators and a dozen congressmen discussing various issues in a film shot at supermarkets, construction sites, and other locations.

In 1971, the networks offered the leadership in Congress an hour of prime time to respond to the State of the Union message. Senator Mansfield appeared alone, interviewed by correspondents from the commercial networks and public broadcasting. CBS, NBC, and public television carried him simultaneously from 10:00 to 11:00 P.M. on January 26; ABC carried him the next day. In 1972, for the first time, the majority leadership of Congress obtained from the networks simultaneous network time to respond to the State of the Union message. Prime time was not requested because the leadership thought it was asking too much. The networks at first resisted simultaneity, but in the end consented. The program was broadcast at 12:30 P.M. on a Friday and showed four Democratic senators and five congressmen delivering prepared statements on domestic issues and answering questions telephoned in from listeners. Speaker Carl Albert and House Majority Leader Hale Boggs also appeared.

During the first thirty months of the Nixon administration, the only television time that Congress could obtain other than its responses to the State of the Union messages was twenty-five minutes that ABC and NBC gave to Senate Majority Leader Mike Mansfield to respond to a presidential address on the economy. The networks turned down Carl Albert when he asked to respond to a televised presidential veto message. The television time for all individuals who might be considered spokesmen for Congress has not approached presidential television in terms of control over format or potential audience (see Appendix A, Table 10).

To a large extent, however, Congress's growing television disadvantage is due to its own failure to utilize fully the opportunities that are available. While Congress as an entity has permitted cameras on the floor at the State of the Union message and on other ceremonial occasions, it has never allowed true broadcast of *deliberations* during Senate or House sessions. The reasons for this refusal are presumably that "the camera will make actors out of members and that the congressional bodies are not ready to suffer the embarrassments which will surely develop when only three or four senators are sitting at their desks reading newspapers while one member of the body is addressing a limited number of disinterested colleagues." [31] The broadcast networks have expressed interest in gaining access to the floor of Congress for filmed, taped, or live coverage of its sessions and debates. The networks would particularly welcome the opportunity to cover special debates and roll calls, although such events do not occur regularly.

The impact of television coverage of Congress's activities has been demonstrated by the televising of congressional hearings. The first televised congressional hearings were broadcast in 1947 from the House Labor Committee. The next year, television showed the nation the tense meeting between Alger Hiss and Whittaker Chambers before the House Committee on Un-American Activities. In 1951, however, the political impact of televised hearings became clear. That year, 20 to 30 million people saw the hearings of the Senate Crime Investigating Committee chaired by Senator Estes Kefauver, who was catapulted into national prominence and almost overnight became a leading contender for the presidency.

In 1954, one-third of the adult population of America saw Senator Joseph McCarthy at least once during the thirty-five days of Senate committee hearings into the dispute between McCarthy and the Army. At one point the Army's counsel, Joseph Welch, turned to McCarthy and said, "Have you no sense of decency, sir? At long last? Have you left no sense of decency?" [32] That arraignment, and McCarthy's own behavior on camera, finished McCarthy. By the end of the year, he had been censured by the Senate.

Televised congressional hearings have helped change public opinion on issues as well as people. Live coverage of Senate Foreign Relations Committee hearings in 1966 showed congressional critics of the president's Vietnam policy and may have increased public opposition to the Vietnam War. James Reston of the *New York Times* observed that the hearings temporarily enabled the president's congressional opponents to influence foreign policy. [33]

Although NBC and ABC carried the hearings live, CBS chose not to, a decision that led to the much-publicized resignation of Fred Friendly as president of CBS News. CBS had carried the live testimony of both David Bell, who supported the administration's Vietnam policies, and General James Gavin, who opposed them. The network kept the antiadministration testimony of former ambassador George Kennan off the network to make room for the fifth rerun of an "I Love Lucy" show and the eighth rerun of "The Real McCoys." CBS chose not to carry Kennan's testimony attacking the U.S. presence in Vietnam live. Friendly called the decision an abdication of the network's responsibility.[34]

Television coverage of the hearings of the Senate Select Committee investigating the Watergate affair brought home to millions the grim details of illegal political campaign tactics and other improper activities directed from the White House. Many committee sessions were covered live by all three commercial networks; others were broadcast live by one network on a rotating basis with the other two. The Public Broadcasting Service videotaped each daytime session for broadcast during evening prime-time hours. While the president's prestige dipped with each day of testimony before the committee, the committee's most articulate and photogenic members were added to the list of possible future presidential candidates.

Despite the potential impact of television events—or perhaps because of it—from 1952 until late 1970 (except for a one-year policy reversal in 1953) the House of Representatives had prohibited broadcast coverage of any of its functions.

In October 1970, under provisions of a House Reorganization Act, broadcasters were given the opportunity to broadcast House committee hearings but only with the approval of the committee chairman or a majority of the committee.[35] Not all committee chairmen have eagerly seized the chance to open their meetings to television. *Broadcasting* magazine has reported that among the committees that were "more than leisurely" in admitting television was the House Interstate and Foreign Commerce

Committee, which deals with legislative matters relating to the broadcast industry.[36]

The first television coverage of a House committee hearing under the new rules took place in February 1971, when all three networks filmed former presidential counselor Daniel Moynihan's testimony on a bill before the Select Subcommittee on Education of the House Education and Labor Committee. The following week, television covered Secretary of the Treasury John Connally's testimony on the federal budget and a proposed extension of the president's wage-price authority before the House Appropriations and Banking and Currency Committees. Since then the networks have filmed numerous excerpts from House hearings. Later in 1971, National Public Radio (the radio counterpart to television's Public Broadcasting Service) initiated live coverage of Congress by carrying a week-long hearing on the rules governing publication of classified material, a hearing prompted by the publication of the "Pentagon Papers" in major U.S. newspapers.

On occasion, the broadcast networks do offer congressional leaders the opportunity to present congressional views in television time comparable to that always available to the president. Early in the Nixon administration, ABC offered to give congressional leaders one hour of prime time at the beginning of the session and another at the end to express their views on the goals, accomplishments, and failures of the session, dividing the two hours between Democrats and Republicans in proportion to their respective strength in Congress. In exchange, ABC asked for permission to cover key congressional debates live during the session. ABC reports that it received no response.

In 1970, NBC made a similar offer by telegram to the leadership of both parties in Congress, offering to produce two programs presenting the views of the majority and minority parties in Congress. The Republican congressional leadership made no response at all. The Democrats insisted that only the majority views—that is, their own—should be broadcast. When the network made time available for congressional response to the 1971 presidential State of the Union address, Senate Majority Leader Mike Mansfield appeared and, visibly ill at ease, opened his remarks by saying he had not wanted to appear but had been the only one willing to do it.[37] The Congress seems generally unwilling to accommodate its procedures to television.

The few congressional initiatives in television either have been unsuccessful or have not been pursued. As early as 1929, Senator Gerald Nye of North Dakota unsuccessfully suggested that Congress build itself a giant transmitter in the District of Columbia and broadcast its views to the nation—a sort of talking *Congressional Record*. In 1961, the Republican congressional leadership initiated its own weekly news conference to respond to President Kennedy's televised press conferences. These conferences, run by Senator Everett Dirksen and House Minority Leader Charles Halleck, came to be called "The Ev and Charlie Show." But the program met with mixed reviews and diminishing returns. The film clips from "The Ev and Charlie Show" that were shown on evening newscasts tended to feature Dirksen's humor rather than his serious opposition to Kennedy's policies. Within a year after the weekly news conferences began, attendance and coverage by reporters had dropped off considerably; the day after a Kennedy conference attended by nearly four hundred reporters, only seventeen newsmen appeared at "The Ev and Charlie Show." The effort was abandoned in 1963.

In 1971, Representative Lester Wolff, a New York Democrat who had worked in television before being elected to Congress, devised a weekly television series called "Ask Congress," which was sold at cost to stations across the country. The broadcasts, produced in the House television studio, featured two or more congressmen from both parties each week, answering questions about Congress sent in by listeners. The Speaker of the House and the Minority Leader of the House were scheduled to appear on the show once every three months. But the show's impact was slight; two years after the first broadcast, only five of the nation's 892 television stations were carrying it.

A year earlier, Senator Fulbright had sponsored a resolution requiring broadcasters to provide network time at least four times a year for broadcasts by "authorized representatives" of the Senate and the House.[38] Fulbright said: "As matters now stand, the President's power to use television in the service of his policies and opinions has done as much to expand the powers of his office as would a constitutional amendment formally abolishing the co-equality of the three branches of Government." [39] The Fulbright resolution provided not only for television responses by Congress after presidential television appearances but also for televised reports initiated by either or both houses of Congress. It did not specify the format or the method of selecting the "authorized representatives"; Fulbright apparently believed the majority and minority leaders in the two houses could work them out.

Before introducing the resolution, Fulbright and his staff had considered a number of other devices: making network time available periodically directly to the majority and minority leaders of both houses; providing the congressional leadership of each party or the party caucuses with reply time within a specified period after a presidential television appearance dealing with matters before Congress; allowing senators or congressmen to secure television time by petition to the networks; creating television response time for any member of Congress who was criticized by the president on television.

Hearings on the Fulbright resolution produced two hundred pages of testimony from broadcasters, senators, and representatives of the two major parties. The broadcasters were united in their opposition to the resolution, asserting that it was tantamount to legislating what viewers would see and hear on television. Frank Stanton of CBS testified that the resolution "affronts at least the spirit of the First Amendment" guaranteeing freedom of speech and that it represented abandonment of Congress's traditional, "wise" opposition to government "interference" with program content and selection. Julian Goodman, president of NBC, testified that "it is inadvisable and undemocratic to establish legislative or regulatory formulas that tell a news medium how it must operate in reporting and analyzing political issues." [40] W. Theodore Pierson, legal counsel for the Republican National Committee, called the resolution impractical and unworkable and said it would open the doors to a legislated governmental right of access to television, "a new and radical concept" in violation of the free press tradition.[41]

Joining Fulbright in support of the resolution were Senators Goodell and Muskie. Both emphasized the power of television in forming public opinion and the imbalance between presidential and congressional access to the nation's television audience. Goodell said:

> The Constitution provides that the Executive and Legislative branches of our government are equal, but the technology of television has shifted the balance. We must arrive at a system whereby there can be a rational confrontation of ideas on the television medium, not Presidential domination of the airways and diffuse responses by different spokesmen on the major issues.[42]

Joseph Califano of the DNC supported the Fulbright resolution, testifying that Congress, "as a coequal branch of the Government, must have access to television in a format that the Congress determines." [43] But the Fulbright resolution never went beyond the hearing stage.

Another 1970 proposal—made by the Republican leader,

Senator Hugh Scott, and William Springer, the senior minority member of the House committee that oversees broadcasting— that all television stations should broadcast a minimum of four special prime-time sessions of Congress each year, died in committee. In 1971 Republican Senate Whip Robert Griffin reintroduced this proposal during the closing days of the 91st Congress; it, too, died in committee. Early in the 92nd Congress, Griffin futilely introduced a resolution to permit live television coverage of Senate floor debate. None of these efforts to obtain greater television access for Congress has been fully supported by Congress itself.

Congress's lack of interest in countering presidential television is surprising in light of its members' keen awareness of broadcasting's effectiveness in increasing their individual political power. Like the early presidential broadcasts, early radio reports by members of Congress impressed the public more with their novelty than with their substance. An early radio address delivered by Senator Clarence Dill from a moving railroad train brought him only telegraphed congratulations for "your moving address." [44] But by 1929, members of Congress were making more than one hundred radio speeches, discussing every important piece of legislation before the 71st Congress.

In 1935, Louisiana Senator Huey Long became a leader of anti-Roosevelt forces in the Senate. A flamboyant personality, Long was an entertaining radio figure who attracted large audiences. Broadcasters were eager to give him free air time; during one two-week period, Long was given three time segments on NBC alone. He often began his broadcasts by asking listeners to telephone friends and tell them to listen, too. He nicknamed himself "the Kingfish," after a well-known character from the "Amos 'n Andy" radio program.

Long used radio broadcasts to spread the gospel of populism and to organize local chapters of his Share-the-Wealth movement. Share-the-Wealth called for the redistribution of large private fortunes in order to provide a $5,000 lump sum for everyone, a guaranteed annual income, shorter work hours, and old-age pensions. By mid-1935, the movement had some eight thousand local chapters across the country, a significant power base from which Long was preparing to mount a campaign against Roosevelt in the 1936 election; but in September 1935 he was assassinated. He was probably the first member of Congress who used radio successfully to make himself a national figure.[45]

One of Long's contemporaries, Representative William Lemke of North Dakota, 1936 presidential nominee of the Union Party, also made radio broadcasts to generate pressure on fellow members of Congress to vote for measures he favored. These efforts resulted in House passage of his bankruptcy legislation.[46]

In 1935, congressmen established a radio recording studio in the House Office Building. There congressmen and senators could record messages for broadcast back in their home constituencies. Today there are six recording rooms in the House studio—one for film, one for videotape, and four for radio. In 1956, the Senate established its own studio.

Which senators and congressmen use the studios and how often are closely guarded secrets. But from April through June 1971, members of the House made more than 101,000 minutes —the equivalent of 70 days—of radio recordings in the House studios. They also made some 172 hours of videotape and 12 hours of film. About 75 percent of congressmen are said to have used the recording facilities at some time, with usage heaviest shortly before the biennial elections. Each congressman must supply his own tape but he can acquire raw film from the studio's stock; equipment and technical personnel are also available as needed. In 1968, the cost of making a five-minute film in the Congressional studios was reported as $12, instead of the several hundred dollars it would cost if produced commercially.[47]

There have been reports that the Republican National Committee maintains a fund of about $50,000 per month for use of Republican members of the Senate and House in the production of television tapes. The tapes are sent to home-state television stations. According to one report, twenty-two senators and dozens of representatives had made use of the television tape money by early 1972.[48]

Individual senators and congressmen can also gain access to both local and national audiences by making themselves available for interviews with newsmen in House and Senate radio-television galleries. The Senate news gallery has one film studio and four radio studios and operates independently of the Senate Recording Studio. In 1968, the most recent year for which figures are available, 1,140 radio interviews and 751 filmed TV interviews were made in the Senate gallery—an average of more than one interview every three weeks for each senator.[49] The rate of interviews on the House side is even higher. Sometimes the House gallery's four television studios and eight radio booths are so busy that congressmen are lined up, waiting their turn to talk with newsmen. Three or four film crews are busy in the House gallery on a typical day, and network crews are present when there is a major vote in the House. Fifteen to twenty radio correspondents are in the gallery daily, interviewing congressmen for regional radio.

The interviews taped in House or Senate facilities are often presented as news clips in local evening radio and television news back home. A leader of Congress, particularly a senator, may often appear on the national network news. When Congress is in session, few network television news programs fail to carry at least one story featuring a congressman or Senator. The story may be about an important vote that day, a committee hearing, or the congressional reaction to a major news event. Television viewers frequently see short film clips of senators or congressmen answering newsmen's questions.

Congressmen and senators can use a variety of means to get

maximum exposure for their views on network television. CBS newsman Marvin Kalb once reported on Senator Fulbright's efforts to gain attention for a major speech on the Middle East. Four days before he delivered the speech, Fulbright made copies available to a select group of reporters. The next day he filmed an interview with three network news commentators for their Saturday evening network news shows. On the following day, a Sunday, he appeared on NBC's "Meet the Press," again discussing his views on the Middle East; his comments were reported on the Sunday newscasts and in Monday morning papers, hours before the speech was finally made on the floor of the Senate. Kalb called what Fulbright had done "an important lesson in the interaction of the Congress and the press" and said it could be interpreted as an example of skillful manipulation of the news media or as a necessary process designed to meet the needs of the public, press, and senator.[50] In spite of the skill he displayed in this instance, Fulbright has stated that:

> One of the things I suffer from, I'm sure all members do, is the feeling that no matter what you do there is no way to communicate it to the people, generally, so that they can understand what you are talking about.[51]

Senator John Pastore has lamented that a senator "has to stand on [his] head in order to get television attention," [52] and Representative Lester Wolff has complained that after a meeting with North Vietnamese representatives in Paris he and other congressmen were able to get news coverage "only through ingenuity." [53] Senator William Proxmire once complained that although four television newsmen arrived to cover his hearings on federal tax loopholes for the rich, three of them soon fell fast asleep. Proxmire was frustrated at the difficulty he had experienced in getting press coverage of committee discussions of important issues. Representative Torbert Macdonald claims that a congressman "has to fire a bomb before television pays attention." [54] The legislator who has neither the taste nor the talent for press-agentry is at a disadvantage.

Network television news coverage of members of Congress differs greatly from news coverage of the president. The news clips are likely to be short, and the congressman does not control the format. The network editors may pass over those remarks that the congressman wished most to stress for something he said that seemed to them more newsworthy. As Senator Fulbright has commented:

> The news spots give us a moment of glorious recognition and, with luck, may even convey a fragment or two of our thinking on some public issues. As likely as not it will be an extraneous fragment, but at least we are given the chance to make a contribution to public discussion—even if it isn't exactly the contribution we would have liked to make.[55]

On the Sunday interview programs—"Meet the Press," "Face the Nation," and "Issues and Answers"—senators and representatives are among the most frequent participants. But audiences for these programs are small, and the format is sometimes stultifying. Senator Fulbright has called the interview programs a "modern, somewhat less lethal equivalent of the Roman arena" in which "journalistic lions" try "to provoke the politician into an indiscretion or maneuver him into a contradiction." [56] Interviewers do not defer to senators and congressmen as they do to the president; thus interviews with congressmen do not provide them with media access comparable to the president's, even though the formats seem similar. Moreover, during the first eighteen months of the Nixon administration, congressmen and senators barely outnumbered executive branch officials by a three to two margin on CBS's "Face the Nation." [57]

The absence of an institutional effort by Congress itself to counter presidential television has given rise to attempts by individual members or small groups of legislators to seek time themselves to speak as spokesmen for what they perceive as a congressional viewpoint on an issue addressed by the president. But the networks have resisted either giving or selling time for this purpose and their resistance has been upheld by the FCC.

During the heat of the conflict between President Nixon and Congress over the president's handling of the Vietnam conflict, senators George McGovern and Mark Hatfield introduced a legislative amendment to a pending appropriations measure as a means of ending U.S. military involvement in Vietnam. The next evening, President Nixon gave a three-network, nation-wide, prime-time television address announcing the incursion into Cambodia and defending continued military involvement in Southeast Asia. The following day, Senator McGovern asked each of the three networks to give or sell him time to urge the public to support his end-the-war amendment instead of the president's policy. CBS and ABC refused. NBC agreed to sell him a half hour for about $60,000 cash in advance.

With a bipartisan group of thirteen other senators and the Amendment to End the War Committee, McGovern purchased the NBC time and spoke to an audience of almost 6 million people. Senators Hatfield, Goodell, Harold Hughes and Frank Church appeared with him. They urged viewers to support the McGovern-Hatfield amendment and to send contributions to pay for the program. Although the program reached only 9.1 percent of television homes—presidential three-network tele-casts commonly reach more than 50 percent—the program brought in about $400,000, far more than it cost.[58] (The re-mainder was used on antiwar propaganda, including television spots.)

In the months that followed, McGovern again asked the net-works to give or sell time to the senators for additional presen-tations in support of war-ending legislation. After President Nixon was featured in an hour-long prime time "Conversation" on ABC, CBS, and NBC, during which he criticized the activities of the McGovern group, McGovern sent telegrams to the three networks requesting equal time to present his and other senators' views in their own way. All three networks rejected his request, saying that they were already covering all sides of the Vietnam controversy in news and public affairs broadcasts. The reply from CBS added that:

> Views on controversial issues can be more objectively presented to our viewers—with maximum opportunity for discussion of the issues in depth and for access by those with differing opinions—if they are covered in our news and public affairs broadcasts rather than in broadcasts prepared and presented by committed partisans.[59]

The fourteen senators and the Amendment to End the War Committee then asked the FCC to require the networks to provide broadcast time for "any substantial group of senators" opposing the president's televised views on a controversial issue of national importance.[60] The senators maintained that this was the only way to redress the television imbalance between the president and Congress, an imbalance which, they said, violated the fairness doctrine. The FCC refused, arguing that the fairness doctrine ran only to issues, not spokesmen or institutions. While the McGovern request was pending at the FCC, eleven Republican senators complained to the FCC that NBC refused to give them time to respond to the McGovern response to the president.[61] The FCC denied this request too.

In 1972, thirteen black congressmen, members of the Black Caucus, unsuccessfully attempted to persuade the networks to provide them with television time to respond to the president. They then filed a petition at the FCC asking the FCC to rule that the three television networks must make "available an appropriate number of prime-time hours," generally an amount comparable to the time given to members of the executive branch of the government, "for direct, unfiltered political speech under the exclusive control" of members of the Senate or House. The Black Caucus request argued that the constitutional doctrine of "separation of powers" required that the networks make time available to the legislative branch. The group suggested that, as a beginning, each of the networks make available "at least one hour a month" of prime television time apportioned among congressional speakers on a reasonable and nondiscriminatory basis. This apportionment could be made either by the television networks or by the Congress itself.[62]

That same year, seven senators and seven congressmen petitioned the FCC to order the television networks to sell or make available for members of Congress broadcast time to present information to the public about matters under consideration by Congress. The Senators and Congressmen had sought to present a program dealing with Vietnam issues then before Congress but had been unable to purchase time from the networks. They urged the FCC to find that their inability to secure network broadcast of their program was inconsistent with the constitutional doctrine of checks and balances. Once again, little support for this or the Black Caucus effort was voiced by congressional leadership, and once again the FCC denied the congressional requests, repeating that only "ideas," not organizations, must be given access to the broadcast media. Viewpoints on Vietnam, said the FCC, had been presented by members of Congress and many others on network news and interview programs. If Congress itself felt it needed a right of access, it could create one by statute, but the FCC felt continued reliance on network judgment to be preferable.[63]

Despite the efforts of individual congressmen, and despite the successes of some legislators in getting on news or interview programs, the public's opportunity to view Congress as an institution in no way compares to its exposure to presidential television. Congress needs television as much as the opposition party does if it is to function as a viable counterweight to the powers of the presidency. "For Congress to meet its full constitutional obligations to the electorate," one of its members has said, "television must become part of the congressional formula." [64] Congress needs television to prevent complete presidential usurpation of legislative initiative—to place programs before the public and to secure public support for its opposition to presidential programs.[65] Congress also needs television to offer yet another viewpoint on national issues. The winding course of political party positions on the Vietnam conflict, for example, indicates that opposition party television may not always encompass the dissenting views of Congress. In addition to the party, therefore, Congress must have sufficient television exposure to play a meaningful role in public debate of national direction.

Yet the nature of Congress weighs against the likelihood that it could present to the public a single television spokesman or position on current issues. The inability of Congress to take advantage of the television opportunities that have been available is an indication of this difficulty. Congress is an institution of enormous diversity, where widely varying positions are slowly, through long hours of proposal and counterproposal, compacted into the majority necessary for passage of legislation. Leadership roles in Congress may require different skills than does an effective television presentation. The Senate majority and minority leaders and the Speaker of the House are not chosen for their television presence but rather for their cloakroom expertise, and the functioning of the institution might well be impeded were the basis for the choices changed. These factors suggest that the allocation of valuable network television time for congressional replies to the president is not likely to be useful to the public or beneficial to Congress.

Congress appears as an institution, as the sum of its individual members, only when it is in session. Just as the opposition party is functioning as a check on presidential power when it runs a candidate against the incumbent, the Congress is performing its function when it is in session investigating, debating, adopting, or rejecting legislative measures. As an institution, it can also be seen and heard with relative ease. Congress exists publicly; its functions take place within a recognizable geographical location at predetermined periods. Anyone sitting in the Senate and House galleries during final debate on a measure will know as well as can be known the "position of Congress" on the matter at issue. This characteristic suggests the manner in which Congress's television access is to be improved. Congress in consultation with the television networks, should permit television cameras on the floor of the House and Senate for the broadcast of specially scheduled prime-time evening sessions at which the most important matters before it each term are discussed, debated, and then voted upon. The sessions should be scheduled and broadcast at least four times per year and carried simultaneously by the networks. The networks' simultaneous broadcast of Congress's response to the president's State of the Union address in 1972 established a precedent for doing the same with special evening sessions.

Special sessions for broadcast could be structured by Congress in any way it believes would be appropriate, perhaps by dividing debate time between the two major political parties in Congress or between recognized positions on the issue under discussion. The division of time, limitation of speakers, and other procedural aspects of debate are matters handled often by Congress and are well within its expertise. Coverage of such events without causing disruption is well within the abilities of the television networks. One well-known figure in the television news field has said that if this suggestion is adopted, it would create one of the most exciting programming possibilities in years.[66] In England, the political parties and the BBC have long agreed upon the amounts of campaign television to be made available each year; in this country, with reasonable effort from both sides, Congress and the networks should have little difficulty agreeing on scheduling, frequency, and production details of congressional television sessions.

Opposition to live television coverage of congressional debates generally has been based upon the argument that cameras would influence some members' behavior—cause them to play to the cameras; that the networks would end up controlling various aspects of congressional proceedings much as they control some professional sports events; that photogenic legislators would have an advantage; that television lights and equipment would make the session physically uncomfortable and disrupt procedures. Yet live television coverage is a fact of life and of government today and the advantages it offers are too important to Congress's vitality to be passed by any longer for any of these reasons.

If a congressman's behavior is "different" before the camera, it is at least an aspect of his character that is on public display, and, in any case, such behavior is likely to decrease as the novelty wears off. Without television, he may not be seen at all, remaining completely beyond public scrutiny. In a democracy, an elected representative functioning before a national audience, even only when he is on his best behavior, is an improvement over one operating out of sight.

There is no reason why some congressional procedures should not be revised to accommodate television; the fact is that television coverage may be more important to Congress's vitality than many age-old rules of procedure. The office of the presidency has made changes to make better use of television, why should not Congress?

If television sessions would give an unnatural advantage to the photogenic member of Congress, they would also give a large audience to the more obscure and less charismatic legislators. As things stand now, it is the legislator who does well with television who already appears most often on interview programs and the evening news. The effective debater, it is

124   PRESIDENTIAL TELEVISION

true, may have an advantage, but it is an advantage to which he is entitled in a deliberative body.

Finally, the fear that television equipment will disrupt congressional sessions is a hangover from the early days of television. Advances in equipment design today make TV surprisingly unobtrusive. Given a chance, the networks could quickly demonstrate their ability to operate on the floor of Congress without great physical annoyance.

To increase broadcaster acceptance in prime time, congressional sessions should be considered exempt from the "equal time" requirement.[67] The "equal time" provision already includes an exemption for news documentaries in which a candidate's appearance is incidental to the major subject; this exemption appears broad enough to include the special sessions. Likewise, to avoid the possibility that special televised sessions might result in an outbreak of "fairness" disputes at the FCC and the imposition of unreasonable obligations on the broadcast industry, special coverage should be exempt from the fairness doctrine. The discussion of a controversial issue during such sessions should not require balancing in the broadcasters' programming on that issue; nor should it cure any previously existing imbalance. Although this might cause some unfairness from time to time, the congressional debates themselves would be likely to be balanced. It would be incongruous to require the broadcast networks to balance the proceedings of the national legislature.

Televised special sessions would provide Congress with simultaneous network prime time largely under its own control. They would allow the institution to put its best face forward; it need not have only a few spokesmen but could rather present all the best voices for or against the important measures, whether proposed by the president or not. Not only the congressional leadership but also members who are expert on various issues could be featured; the issues could cover the vast range of business before Congress, rather than being limited to a rebuttal to a presidential appearance. Frank Stanton of CBS has agreed that these sessions would be "the most effective and truest way to present [Congress] as a countervailing force to the Presidency. . . . This would reveal its pluralistic character rather than abridge it." [68] The live broadcast of congressional sessions would be effective television for the vast majority of Americans who have never had an opportunity to see Congress in action. Television coverage of a few special sessions annually might be only a beginning. Congress might later on decide to allow television onto the floor of the House and Senate permanently. Coverage of all sessions would result in more congressional appearances on television news, in network "specials," in live broadcasts on important occasions, and in weekly summaries of the proceedings.

Congress was intended to be a representative institution whose proceedings would be public to the greatest possible extent. The Constitution, in fact, requires that a journal of proceedings be kept and published, a requirement intended "to insure publicity to the proceedings of the legislature." [69] Legislators today would not think of banning newspaper reporters from their sessions. Most legislators have opposed proposals that they be wholly insulated from the public galleries for safety's sake. Yet, newspapers no longer are the prime source of the public's news, and the galleries are obviously too small and too distant for most people. To be public today means to be on television. Presidents know this and behave accordingly. To balance the president, Congress should go public too.

CHAPTER 5

THE
LOYAL OPPOSITION

THE ULTIMATE CHECK on a president is the possibility that the opposition party may beat him or his party at the next election. "In our democratic system," a party leader observes, the political party has carried "the major burden of defining and debating national policy." [1] Every president has had to weigh his policies against opposition challenge.

Yet the opposition party is not always the most effective opposition on a particular issue. A lack of policy-making machinery, a lack of a designated spokesman, the practical politics of some questions, may prevent the party from mounting a challenge to a particular presidential policy. Throughout most of the Johnson administration, for example, the Republican party's position on the Vietnam War did not differ significantly from the Democratic party's. True, some individual Democrats and Republicans opposed Johnson's Vietnam policy. But by and large, the most outspoken opposition came from such organizations as the Business Executives Move, the Women's Strike for Peace, and other *ad hoc* groups. In the history of broadcasting, the most effective opposition to administration policy has come from such sources rather than from the major opposition party as such. In the 1930s, CBS and Mutual gave radio time to a group of businessmen to broadcast what they called "Crusader" programs attacking the New Deal.[2] CBS also carried "The Ford Sunday Evening Hour," sponsored by Ford Motor Company, featuring classical music interlaced with speeches by company executives eulogizing Henry Ford and attacking the New Deal.

Perhaps the most intensive use of broadcasting to attack presidential policies was made by Father Charles E. Coughlin in the 1930s. Coughlin originally bought time on a Detroit radio station to solicit funds for his small church. Finding that his broadcast attacks on wealth, power, and capitalism elicited a flood of letters and contributions, he expanded his purchases to stations across the country. When CBS, alarmed at some of Coughlin's rhetoric, asked him to submit scripts in advance, Coughlin used a radio broadcast to tell his listeners that he was being censored, and CBS received more than a million letters of protest from Coughlin followers. By late 1932, Coughlin was purchasing time on twenty-six radio stations to denounce President Hoover and an alleged conspiracy of international bankers. A Philadelphia poll indicated that listeners preferred Father Coughlin's broadcasts to a New York Philharmonic Orchestra concert by fifteen to one. When Roosevelt took office, Coughlin assailed him, too. Coughlin's programs opposing the president's proposal to join the World Court in 1934 resulted in so many telegrams protesting the president's position that they had to be brought into Washington by train from Baltimore.[3]

One of the most memorable broadcasts in opposition to presidential policy was the television address delivered by Clarence Randall of the Inland Steel Company in April 1952. President Truman had announced that because of the inability of union and management to settle a labor dispute threatening the economy, the federal government would take over operation of the steel industry. Randall asked for and received television time to deliver a scathing attack on the Truman position:

> I have a deep sense of responsibility as I face this vast audience of the air. I am here to make answer on behalf of the steel industry to charges flung over these microphones last night by the man who then stood where I stand now. I am a plain citizen. He was the President of the United States.
>
> Happily we still live in a country where a private citizen may look the President in the eye and tell him that he was wrong. . . .[4]

With the help of the courts, and perhaps this appearance, Randall and the steel industry prevailed.

As election time draws near, however, it is the party out of power, rather than any individual, that devises a platform of opposition to the party in power and its leader, the president. Because it is one of but two (sometimes three) major organizations that every four years place a candidate for president before the electorate, the opposition party becomes a focus for all those opposed to the policies of the incumbent. Although minor parties from time to time have been important, their function usually resembles that of the *ad hoc* issue-oriented organizations, framing opposition positions for the major opposition party to adopt, rather than presenting a candidate who represents a serious threat to the incumbent. The winning presidential candidate is, on the whole, accepted as party leader and party spokesman for the next four years, although some members of his party in Congress may oppose him on some issues. The incumbent president ordinarily controls the national party committee and, through patronage, other levels of the party organization. He can use his access to television to mobilize public opinion behind himself and his party. As the Democratic National Committee sees them, "the networks are . . . at the call of the President, to permit him to use the nation's airwaves to lay the groundwork for his reelection on hour after hour of prime time television." [5] CBS has said that presidential television "seeks to perpetuate [the presidential] party's stewardship of the government." [6]

The party that loses the presidential election has no comparable leader. The defeated presidential candidate does not necessarily retain his position as party spokesman. Often opposition party leadership devolves upon the party's congressional delegation. But the congressional leadership may be fragmented, especially as the next election nears and congressmen vie once more for the presidential nomination. The American opposition party has no shadow cabinet as has the British opposition. And although from time to time an American opposition party has attached a study group on issues to its national committee, the members of that group are not authorized representatives of the party's elected government officials, party hierarchy, or voters registered as party members. The Democratic Advisory Council of the 1950s, for example, was constantly at odds with the Democratic leadership in Congress. The opposition party's national committee has devoted its energy not to policy making but to fund-raising, providing logistic support for local campaigns, and preparing for the next presidential campaign. At their headquarters in Washington, the national party committees develop political research, distribute party information, handle public relations, try to coordinate party committees and organizations and officeholders, assign party members as public speakers, and raise money.[7] They are not responsible for formulating or speaking on behalf of party positions. Indeed, the Republican National Committee itself has denied that committee members are "appropriate spokesmen to discuss specific political, economic, and social issues." [8] The 1968 Democratic manual stated explicitly that the policy proposals of the national committee "carry no official mandate." [9]

The opposition party's leaders frequently disagree on issues. The Democratic National Committee, attempting to respond to President Nixon's televised addresses on Vietnam but afraid to slight any of the party's potential candidates, squeezed all of them into the committee's few television programs, thus diluting their impact. The party's quest for a consensus resulted in a watered-down response that George Reedy, President Johnson's former press secretary, said "sounds like yapping" to most television viewers.[10] Similarly, the Republican party was internally divided in its opposition to President Johnson's Vietnam policies, some members favoring escalation and others a settlement. "There are no parties for all practical purposes," says Fred Dutton, "only factions and power struggles. A party is only a loose abstraction." [11] This seems overstated—but it makes a point.

Yet, if every appearance of the president on television has political significance, if the president can be regarded as campaigning throughout his term, then it is essential that the opposition party somehow maintain the ability to compete. It is not only diffuseness, lack of structure, and lack of a preeminent leader or a single line on issues that have limited the opposition party's effectiveness in responding to presidential television. Lack of comparable access to television severely compounds the opposition's difficulty.

Table 9 sets forth all network television appearances of individuals reasonably viewed as opposition party spokesmen during the first thirty months of the Nixon administration. The list includes the defeated presidential and vice-presidential candidates, leading announced candidates for the presidential nomination in the next election, spokesmen designated by the Democratic National Committee, the chairman of the national committee, and, since the opposition controlled Congress, the Speaker of the House and the Senate majority leader. In prime, simultaneous, three-network television time, the broadcast opportunities represented by this list do not begin to compare with those of the president set forth in Table 7.

Clearly no other single political figure enjoys so much access to television as the president. It has been suggested, however, that in combination the president's political opponents may even have greater exposure than he. President Nixon's press secretary, Ronald Ziegler, believes that the opposition can "collectively—regularly—and with great impact—attack the President's policy. . . . The collective weight of their opposition equals or outweighs the TV statements of the President. It balances without question." [12] Peter Lisagor, the Washington bureau chief of the *Chicago Daily News,* maintains that although the opposition's access to television may come "spasmodically and sporadically," on the whole the opposition party "has a relatively easy crack at television." [13]

It gets its crack most frequently in network news programs. Strenuous opposition to specific administration policies is news. On days when the president takes a controversial action, the evening newscasts almost invariably include at least a brief film clip of an opposition leader's comment. The network news broadcasts on CBS and NBC reach an audience of close to 20 million people, and ABC's audience is not much smaller. On a typical winter evening, more than 40 million homes can be counted on to watch one of the network newscasts.[14] In addition, from time to time network news "specials" display opposition party views or leaders for periods longer than the news film clip.

But news broadcasts or news "specials" can never give the opposition parity with the president. When the president makes a half-hour speech to the people, an opposition leader's response may get a minute or two on the news. Occasionally, network interpretations following a presidential address include an appearance of an opposition leader, but most often he is accompanied by a member of the president's own party. The opposition party cannot control its news appearances as the president controls his television time. What the opposition does not have, above all, is network time to take its case to the people in its own way, not the way a television newsman, commentator, or editor sees it. It can be argued that viewers are likely to be more skeptical of a controlled program than an uncontrolled news broadcast, but the president appears in news broadcasts as well as controlled programs and thus has the advantage of both. In formats that he does not overtly control, the president benefits from the deference his office inspires, an advantage that opposition spokesmen lack.

The weekly network interview programs devote more time to partisan politics than any other television programs. Most of the guests on "Meet the Press" (NBC), "Face the Nation" (CBS), and "Issues and Answers" (ABC) [15] are members of Congress, cabinet officers, state or local elected officials, or White House staff members. During the first thirty months of the Nixon administration most of the opposition party's television appearances took place on these programs.[16] Peter Lisagor, who is a frequent interviewer on the question-and-answer shows, has said that the programs "compete for people and go after the dissenter," largely because the dissenter is likely to be more controversial and a livelier subject for an interview.[17] But administration officials also appear often, because those who plan the interview programs strive to maintain an internal balance that does little to reduce the overall imbalance in access of administration and opposition spokesmen.

In any case, an appearance on an interview program is not a free pass to the nation's living rooms. Nearly all such programs appear in the daytime on Sunday when most people are not sitting home watching television. Broadcasters acknowledge that the chief value of these programs to the networks is not audience or sponsorship but rather the possibility that a guest will say something newsworthy enough to make the front page of Monday's *New York Times* or *Washington Post,* and thus give the network prestige.

In their early days, interview programs were bear-baiting affairs, designed more to embarrass the guest than to elicit information. Even today, the topics to be discussed are chosen by the questioners, not the guest, and often the guest is sharply questioned. The questioner is as interested in his own television image as the guest. By the time the interviewer has asked his questions—and perhaps made statements of his own—and by the time the station-break commercials have been shown, the guest may find himself with considerably less time to expound his own views than the president would have in a similar setting.

The only way that an opposition party spokesman can gain access to television time under his own control is to be given it by the networks or to buy it himself. Occasionally, one of the networks has offered time to the opposition to use as it sees fit. But the networks have never directly given the opposition party simultaneous three-network prime time to present its views and images at a time and in a format chosen by the party—the conditions in which the president operates.[18] From January 20, 1969, through August 1, 1971, President Nixon made fourteen television addresses and held fifteen televised news conferences, all carried simultaneously and free by all three networks, while the opposition party as such made three appearances, none of them broadcast on all networks simultaneously.[19]

Of course, the opposition party can buy time. But a half-hour of simultaneous prime time on all networks can cost over $250,000, more than the opposition should reasonably be expected to spend to balance the president's free appearances. In 1972, it was also more than the Democratic party could afford.

And even if it were not, the networks would probably not be willing to sell the time. The networks are not eager to disrupt program schedules and replace proven audience-drawing programs with a political lecture. They also fear complaints from sponsors whose commercial messages may happen to appear immediately before or after a controversial political program. The networks have generally attempted to restrict and discourage the sale of time to a political party for spot announcements on controversial issues except during recognized campaign periods.

It is thus not surprising that in recent years the Democratic National Committee has gone to court to obtain greater access to television. Republican leaders also have privately acknowledged that, had they been out of power since 1969, they would have fought the battles themselves.

At the end of the first year of his administration, President Nixon had made four television addresses carried in prime time simultaneously by all networks, had held eight televised news conferences, and had been supported by more than fifty network appearances [20] of his political allies, including Vice President Agnew, Attorney General Mitchell, and the Republican National Committee chairman. Not once during this period had the Democratic National Committee (DNC) obtained access to network television under its own control. The DNC's views had been expressed only through the occasional appearance of its chairman, Senator Fred Harris of Oklahoma, on non-prime-time interview programs.

When Lawrence O'Brien became chairman of the DNC in March of 1970, he was deeply concerned about the television problem. "Almost from the day I resumed the national chairmanship," O'Brien has said, "The National Committee has had at the top of its agenda a campaign to redress the imbalance that favors the party in power in the matter of access to television and radio." [21] Enlisting the help of Joseph Califano, a former White House assistant under President Johnson and then a partner in the Washington law firm of Arnold and Porter, the DNC began an aggressive legal campaign to obtain television time.

Soon after taking office, O'Brien asked the networks to cover a speech he was to give in Milwaukee responding to the president's policy statements on Indochina. ABC covered the speech live and in prime time, although CBS and NBC carried only brief film clips in their regular newscasts.

In July 1970, CBS offered the DNC time on the new "Loyal Opposition" program. But this advance was abruptly halted by an FCC decision (later reversed by the courts) that time would have to be given the Republicans to respond. With the network chary of further antagonizing the Republicans and unwilling to fight continued battles at the FCC and in the courts, the "Loyal Opposition" went off the air after one program.

The DNC's major effort, at this time, was directed at obtaining spots for fund-raising and brief statements of Democratic positions. Millions of dollars in debt from the 1968 presidential campaign, the DNC believed that success in the 1970 and 1972 elections depended upon a fund-raising effort aimed at attracting large numbers of small contributors. During the 1964 campaign, a single television appeal for funds by the Republican National Committee chairman, Dean Burch, had brought in 70,000 letters and 3,500 money orders. The Republican campaign broadcasts that year had resulted in more than 100,000 contributions under $100 each.[22] In 1968, televised fund solicitations for the Humphrey campaign had produced almost $300,000 in contributions averaging $10 each (though some contributions were far larger). More recently, a televised fund appeal by five senators seeking a legislative end to the Vietnam War had raised more than $100,000 in small contributions. The DNC therefore had concluded that television was the most effective way to reach large numbers of small contributors.

The DNC planned an elaborate television campaign that would include full-length programs as well as spots. Some programs and spots would be devoted to fund solicitation; others would comment on administration policies and offer alternatives. To produce all these programs and announcements the DNC would have to make a sizable initial expenditure of funds, and it hesitated to do so without assurance that it would be able to put its programs and spots on the air.

CBS had rejected earlier DNC bids to purchase time, citing a policy of selling broadcast time for the presentation of political views only during election campaigns. Other stations seemed flatly opposed to selling time for the presentation of views on controversial issues or for the solicitation of funds. Since such policies were so prevalent among the various networks and independent broadcasters, the DNC concluded that "there must be a national uniform communications policy with respect to the activities of a responsible group, such as the DNC, that would permit the kind of access through which funds could be solicited and the American people informed of divergent views on national issues." [23]

The DNC therefore petitioned the FCC to rule that, under the First Amendment to the Constitution and the Communications Act, a broadcaster could not, "as a general policy, refuse to sell time to responsible entities, such as the DNC, for the solicitation of funds and for comment on public issues." The DNC argued that a broadcast licensee's arbitrary refusal to sell time to a political party would be contrary to the public's First Amendment right to receive views and information, would fail to fulfill the FCC's programming requirements, and would indicate that the station was not operating in the "public interest, convenience, and necessity," the statutory standard for keeping a broadcasting license.

The FCC's decision was predictable: because broadcast frequencies were limited, Congress licensed their use on condition that it serve the public interest. Licensees must therefore devote time to controversial issues. But this requirement was based on the right of the public to be informed, rather than the right of individual members of the public to broadcast their own views. With few exceptions, none relevant here, only issues, not individuals or groups, had any right of access to television time.[24]

The FCC also cited its concern that if broadcast access for opposing sides of issues must be sold, coverage of the issues could be distorted by financial considerations. Because the networks had recently promised to sell the DNC time for fund solicitations, the FCC did not rule on the issue of whether such time must be sold; it did suggest, however, that restricting the sale of air time to election periods appeared arbitrary and inconsistent with the public interest.

The DNC then took its case to the United States Court of Appeals, arguing that it was unconstitutional for broadcasters to refuse to sell time to a major political party. Under the First Amendment, it argued, broadcasters could not erect and the FCC could not sanction arbitrary barriers to reasonable access to television against a major political party or other responsible political groups or individuals.[25]

In a decision of considerable significance, a divided Court of Appeals held that a broadcaster's "flat ban on paid public issue announcements is in violation of the First Amendment, at least when other sorts of paid announcements are accepted." [26] The court did not say that the DNC, or any other group, must be allowed to purchase spot time, but it did say that the FCC could not condone a broadcaster's complete ban on sales of advertising time for views on controversial issues. The court acknowledged the importance of broadcasting, particularly broadcast advertising, in exposing public issues and, consequently, the importance of access to broadcasting for the views of a political party. In the American political system, said the court, "it is of obvious importance that the public have access—as direct and full as possible—to the views of the political parties. A party currently out of office may well regard such communication as particularly vital." "Uninhibited, robust, and wide-open" debate could not become a reality on television if individuals or groups had no opportunity to express their views in their own way. One means of providing this opportunity was through paid advertising. The court ordered the FCC to develop regulations to put into effect paid access to television.

The decision seemed to be a significant victory for the DNC and other groups opposing the president's policy. But on May 29, 1973 the Supreme Court, in a split decision, reversed the case and, upholding the FCC, ruled that neither the Communications Act nor the First Amendment required broadcasters to accept particular editorial advertisements. Chief Justice Burger, in his prevailing opinion, upheld the present system of balance between the public interest and broadcasters' journalistic freedom that Congress intended and that is maintained by the FCC and its Fairness Doctrine. A right of access might undermine fairness, he wrote, and involve the government increasingly in regulating or censoring day-to-day broadcasting. It might weigh access heavily in favor of those who were wealthy enough to buy it. It might transfer control from broadcasters who *are* accountable to private individuals who *are not*. Burger said that although many attempts have been made to give individuals the right of access, Congress had not yet seen fit to do so.

This decision not only undid several years' efforts to establish a legal right to buy time but also reversed a recent legal trend in that direction. If a right of access is to be established, Congress will have to act.

While the Democrats were seeking to establish a right to purchase network time, the Republicans presented, on the Friday before the congressional elections of 1970, a network rebroadcast of President Nixon's campaign speech delivered earlier that day in Anaheim, California. The president told the national television audience that the country needed "members of the House and Senate who will vote for the president and not against him, so that we can see to it that the wave of crime does not become the wave of the future in the United States of America." He said that the candidates he was campaigning for —all Republicans—had "not adopted [a] permissive attitude toward either crime or toward this kind of violent protest." [27]

The Democratic National Committee had no money to arrange for a last-minute response to the president's partisan speech, and they had no single national leader to speak for them. But a group of Democrats headed by the DNC general counsel, Joseph Califano, and a former Eugene McCarthy campaigner, Geoffrey Cowan, discussed the possibility of forming a committee to purchase fifteen minutes of time on CBS that Sunday evening. Independent of the DNC, the committee could raise the money and choose the speaker quickly and without consulting all party leaders. Averell Harriman became chairman of the committee. Presently it learned that the Republicans planned to buy time on all three networks to broadcast the tape of another Nixon campaign speech, this one the president's hard-hitting law-and-order speech delivered in Phoenix the Saturday before the election. The networks asked the *ad hoc* committee of Democrats if it wanted to buy time, thus creating two back-to-back broadcasts on election eve—first the Nixon broadcast and then the committee broadcast. The DNC then requested free time on all three networks. The networks refused. Thereupon, Harriman advanced $100,000 toward the $135,000 needed for the fifteen minutes of simultaneous network time. The Republican party paid for the president's fifteen minutes.

On Monday evening, President Nixon appeared on the networks in the edited, black-and-white videotape of his Phoenix speech. He was immediately followed by Senator Edmund Muskie, chosen by the Democratic *ad hoc* committee. Muskie criticized "the Republican tactics of fear and division which threatened to tear our country apart." [28] He said the president lied. Both broadcasts evoked strong public reaction. The Nixon videotape was of such poor quality technically that the networks felt compelled to disclaim responsibility for it. The president spoke in live-audience campaign style. Muskie, seated in his home, spoke softly and directly into the camera. His speech was extremely well received, added to his stature as a leading Democrat, and demonstrated the potential effectiveness of party television presentations.[29]

In 1971, President Nixon increased his use of television. In January, the White House arranged for an hour-long interview of the president on all three networks simultaneously, followed two weeks later by the televised State of the Union message. In February the president delivered a nationwide radio speech. In the next two months, through televised press conferences and interviews, the president appeared on prime-time network television a total of three and one-half hours. On March 15, NBC's "Today" show featured its extraordinary two-hour interview with the president; on March 22, the president gave his hour-long interview with Howard K. Smith of ABC. On April 7 he appeared simultaneously on all three networks to deliver a speech on Southeast Asia.

The confusion and litigation that resulted from the Democratic party's efforts to keep pace with the president, and its overall lack of success, illustrate the absence of any comparable television access for the opposition party. The DNC viewed the Howard K. Smith ABC interview as an "image-building attempt" by the president, noting that the president had discussed the "Nixon doctrine" for Southeast Asia, claimed to spend more of his time in the office than any other president, and defended his veto of a Democratic election reform bill.[30] The president, the DNC said, used the time on ABC virtually to announce his intention to run for reelection in 1972.[31] O'Brien charged that the president, according to his own associates, was using television "to reveal to the American people still another 'new Nixon.' "[32] For these reasons, the DNC asked ABC to make available to it one hour of prime time free.[33] ABC refused, maintaining that it had already treated the issues in a fair and balanced way on news and interview programs.

The DNC viewed the president's two-hour interview on NBC's "Today" program as an opportunity for the president to project a favorable image of himself, and it asked NBC for two free hours on the same program.[34] NBC, however, saw the "Today" interview as "philosophical in nature, rather than a discussion of issues," and as dealing mainly with Mrs. Nixon's influence on her husband's career and the role of women in government and journalism.[35] References to Vietnam, crime, or inflation were so incidental as not to constitute a discussion of controversial issues for fairness doctrine purposes, NBC argued; and even if they did, the issues had been adequately covered by other NBC programs.

A week after NBC turned down the DNC request for time on "Today," the networks provided the president with prime time on all networks to deliver an address on the war in Indochina. The DNC requested comparable network time. O'Brien argued that President Nixon had sought in his address to place the blame for the war "solely on the Democratic party, in a manner that requires a response by the Party's designated spokesman."[36] President Nixon had said, for example:

> When I left Washington in January of 1961, after serving eight years as Vice President under President Eisenhower, there were no American combat forces in Vietnam. No Americans had died in combat.
>
> When I returned as President eight years later, there were 540,000 American troops in Vietnam. Thirty-one thousand had died there. Three hundred Americans were being lost every week. There was no comprehensive plan to end the United States involvement in the war. . . .

Tonight I do not ask you to take what I say in faith. Look at the record: Every action taken by this Administration, every decision made, has accomplished what I said it would accomplish. They have reduced our casualties.[37]

NBC again refused on the grounds that its news and interview programs could provide adequate balance.[38] So did CBS.

At ABC, however, the DNC request had a different reception. Although asserting that its "overall coverage of the Indochina issue has been fair and balanced, complying fully with the requirements of the FCC Fairness Doctrine," ABC agreed that in view of the importance of the war issue, additional coverage at this time would serve the public interest, and offered the DNC one half-hour of prime-time television on April 22, 1971.[39]

The DNC called it a "major breakthrough," the first free television time made available in response to a DNC request in more than two years. Six Democratic senators, all potential presidential candidates, participated in the broadcast, making brief statements urging withdrawal of troops from Vietnam. Chairman O'Brien opened and closed the program.

The Republican National Committee (RNC) promptly asked ABC for time to respond to the Democratic response. As the RNC saw it, the president had addressed the nation on the Vietnam War without partisan recrimination or attempts to blame the war on the Democrats. It was the Democrats who raised the issue of who was responsible for Vietnam, the RNC argued, and in fairness, ABC must give the Republicans time to reply.[40]

ABC argued that it made news judgments in good faith when choosing spokesmen for and methods of presenting varying views and had chosen the DNC on that basis. It also complained of being caught in the middle of partisan sparring:

Thus on one hand we are challenged by the Democrats because they contend we have been unfair to them and on the other hand by the Republicans who say we have been too fair to the Democrats. Such a set of circumstances, which undoubtedly will continue and expand during the months ahead, neatly illustrates the dilemma in which broadcasters are placed in the "gamesmanship" currently underway between the major parties.[41]

The RNC filed a complaint at the FCC, arguing that since ABC's coverage of the war issue had been balanced without the DNC program, the DNC appearance created an imbalance under the fairness doctrine that only an RNC appearance could rectify.[42]

Repeating settled fairness doctrine, the FCC concluded that ABC had given the Democrats time to discuss an issue on which the other side had been presented many times; since the DNC had discussed only that issue, ABC's overall programming was balanced and no time need be made available to the Republican party.[43]

The DNC made good its vow to "pursue every course available." It filed complaints with the FCC against NBC for its failure to provide a response to the "Today" program, against CBS for its denial of time to respond to the president's April address on Indochina, and against ABC for its Smith interview, even though ABC had made time available to the DNC after Nixon's address.

The DNC argued to the FCC that the presidential appearances were tantamount to free television time for the Republicans, and that if such time were given to the Republicans in the period before an election, while the Democrats were covered only in news and interview programs, pursuant to the "political party doctrine," the FCC would be almost certain to hold that the network had not fulfilled its fairness obligation. The DNC described the president's television appearances as having "touted the achievements of his administration," "detailed the accomplishments of his administration," "again placed the blame . . . on the Democratic party," and been "an image-building effort looking toward the 1972 presidential election." The DNC maintained that the president's television appearances marked the beginning of the 1972 presidential campaign and were intended to persuade the people that his personality entitled him to their support in 1972.[44]

The FCC rejected the DNC complaints and refused to consider the president's television appearances as political party appearances to which the political party doctrine would apply.[45] The commission held that only the fairness doctrine applied, and that the overall programming of the three networks was fair on the substantive issues involved. The FCC did not recognize that any political imbalance might be caused by the many television appearances of the leader of one of the two major political parties. The commission took more than four months to reach this conclusion.

As the election year of 1972 began, DNC Chairman Lawrence O'Brien looked forward to "a year of major legal breakthroughs on the broadcasting front." [46] Opposition access to television had turned into an endurance contest, however, with the opposition the loser. The DNC returned to court to appeal the FCC's decision, as did the Republicans, who were determined to respond to any response to the president. The court denied the DNC appeal, holding that the law requires only that the public be adequately informed on issues, not that it receive its information from opposition party leaders.[47]

The denials of DNC requests for television time continued as the presidential election drew closer. The FCC rejected a request that it order the networks to make time available to the DNC to respond to a series of seven appearances beginning in August 1971 by President Nixon and Treasury Secretary Connally outlining new administration economic policy. The FCC again declined to create an "equal time" theory for the opposition political party to respond to the president; it was sufficient, said the commission, that the networks had fairly presented the dispute over the economy in their own way.[48] A few months later the FCC upheld CBS's refusal to provide the Democrats with television time to counter a one-hour interview with President Nixon by Dan Rather, and NBC's refusal of time to match a special "Day in the Life of the President." The FCC again had rejected a contention that there should be an automatic right to respond to presidential appearances by the party out of power.[49]

In the face of the increasing pressure from the DNC and others on its policies and procedures, the FCC had instituted "a broad-ranging inquiry into the efficacy of the fairness doctrine and other Commission public interest policies." [50] The commission invited comment from interested parties on all aspects of fairness in media access, noting that it had been twenty-two years since the last full-fledged investigation of the subject. Among the areas specified for investigation was the application of the fairness concept to political broadcasts. Since current fairness interpretation required broadcasters to sell or give time to one major party if they gave or sold time to the other party, and since this interpretation had not been extended to presidential appearances, the commission sought suggestions on whether the interpretation "should be restricted, expanded, or left alone."

The following year, the FCC concluded its review by declining to revise its approach to presidential television. Instead, the commission suggested that any decision to create "equal time" for the opposition party outside of campaign situations must originate with Congress, not an administrative agency. It urged licensees to be alert to the views of the opposition in making programming decisions under existing fairness principles but once again avoided the question of political, as opposed to issue, imbalance.[51]

The response of broadcasters to this exhortation is not likely to be great. The broadcasters generally believe that they are already transmitting views on all sides of important controversial issues. As they see it, "what is essential is not that everyone shall speak, but that everything worth saying shall be said." [52] And they use minute-by-minute analyses of their programming to prove that radio and television do say everything worth saying about politics and government.

Broadcasters believe that presidential opposition, including the opposition political party, is adequately covered when it is "news" and need not be covered when it is not news.[53] If the opposition party is not so newsworthy as the president, broadcasters say, they are under no obligation to compensate for that natural disadvantage, particularly since the "out" party is heard on interview and panel programs. Ted Pierson, special counsel to the Republican National Committee, believes that television today already fills the air with dissent. He maintains that anyone who claims opposition views on major issues are not available on television "must be deaf, dumb, and blind." [54] Democratic Congressman Torbert H. Macdonald of Massachusetts, whose House Subcommittee on Communications and Power oversees the FCC, also once felt that network news and interview coverage provided an adequate forum for opposition to the president.[55] But in 1973 Macdonald introduced a bill to require broadcasters to provide the opposition party with time to respond to presidential addresses. Without some reform there is little likelihood that opposition party access to television—to the type of television that would allow it to present its leaders and views effectively—will improve.

Lawrence O'Brien, as chairman of the DNC, placed the blame for his party's inability to hold its own against presidential television on "a combination of outmoded laws, FCC regulations and industry practices." [56] Existing laws and regulations have indeed proved inadequate here. As a result, lacking regulatory pressure and believing their performance to be sufficient, television stations and networks have created the problem of presidential television. As presidents have requested more and more television time, broadcasters have given freely, and the corresponding access of the president's political adversaries has fallen dangerously far behind. Today a real question exists whether television is in the process of destroying the opposition's ability to present its case in competition with the president. Clearly there is need for reform. Proposals for reform range from the rather simple, such as moving network interview programs into prime time, to the rather complex, such as creating a separate commission to allocate broadcast time to party spokesmen after any presidential address that the commission might find requires a response. Some proposed reforms would raise greater television exposure to the level of a party "right," with the broadcaster bearing the full practical burden; others would place the burden on the party to make itself "news" before securing access. To some, "access" itself means three-network prime time when and how you want to use it; to others, it means only the availability of news about the party.

Reform of the system must recognize that the opposition party checks the president primarily by posing the possibility that it may defeat him or his party at the next election. It does this by providing logistic support for opposition candidates more than by debating the incumbent on issues. This is why the opposition party, whether Democrat or Republican, is likely to lack a clear spokesman and a clear position on issues except during a presidential election; and this is why it may not be well qualified to present a rapid, direct, and reasoned response to the president during his term. Reform, therefore, must be directed at protecting the party's primarily electoral function, not at giving it time to present its views between elections, when neither a party view nor a party spokesman may exist.

Realistic reform must also recognize that the television audience for political programs is relatively small. Even the president, when he does not appear on all networks simultaneously, attracts smaller audiences than regular network programs. The audience for other political figures is even smaller. The vast American public, if it has a choice, will not choose to watch politicians. Those who do watch probably watch only those politicians with whom they already agree.

Few people would notice and even fewer would complain were political programs taken off the air entirely. While citizen groups have enthusiastically taken up the cause of better children's programs and have vehemently denounced the suggestion that sports events be shown on closed circuit rather than public TV, there has been no trace of public demand for opposition party television. In November 1972, both a scheduled television address by the Democratic presidential candidate, George McGovern, and a professional football game were taken off the air at the last minute. TV stations were inundated with complaints from football fans but received virtually no inquiries about McGovern.[57] More than once, politicians who purchased television time during a campaign have been berated by the public for preempting favorite entertainment shows.

The small audience argues against providing party responses after each presidential address; the politicians are likely to be talking only to themselves. At the same time, political affairs are important to the country, and the opposition party's very utility as an institution is largely dependent upon access to the public. Just as broadcasters have an acknowledged obligation to present news programs even though most viewers might prefer a longer "Laugh In," so do they have an obligation to elevate political discourse by presenting opposition candidates and views to the public.

New opportunities for opposition television should ensure as effective a presentation as possible. Party positions should be made known through party leaders, not only through summations by network commentators or newsmen. On the importance of a direct statement of a position, John Stuart Mill wrote:

> Nor is it enough that he should hear the arguments of adver-
> saries from his own teachers, presented as they state them, and
> accompanied by what they offer as refutations. That is not the
> way to do justice to the arguments, or bring them into real con-
> tact with his own mind. He must be able to hear them from per-
> sons who actually believe them; who defend them in earnest,
> and do their very utmost for them.[58]

The party should have the opportunity to use formats that
effectively present both issues and personalities. Under some
circumstances, the party must appear simultaneously in prime
time on all three networks as does the president. Finally reform
must eliminate FCC control over political broadcasting. The
government administrative process is simply not well suited to
dealing effectively with the changing complexities of politics.
Staff levels have always been too low and processing time too
long to permit rapid decisions. FCC Chairman Burch noted in
1971 that in eight years the number of broadcast complaints
handled by the commission increased fivefold, while staff levels
remained unchanged. "This means substantial backlogs," said
Burch, "and it means that complaints in a number of critical
areas such as the fairness doctrine . . . are not disposed of in a
timely fashion." [59] Complaints alleging broadcast "unfairness"
in October 1972 were ten times higher than in the same month
preceding the 1968 presidential election.[60]

Even with adequate funds and staff, the FCC could not regulate political broadcasting satisfactorily. A headline in *Broadcasting* magazine asks, "Any way to get fairness under control?
Question now is whether FCC, under whatever majority, can
cope with pressure groups, politics and courts." [61] The FCC is
subject to congressional pressures; Congress controls its budget,
can investigate the FCC, and can override FCC decisions with
legislation. When the FCC set out to determine whether restric-
tions should be placed on commercials, congressional hearings
quickly resolved the question. Just so, Congress prevailed when
it differed with the FCC on pay-TV and license renewal procedures.

Moreover, the FCC is also beholden to the president, who appoints its commissioners and chairman, controls spending, and clears legislative proposals through the Office of Management and Budget. During a 1971 Senate committee hearing, Senator Pastore remarked to the FCC chairman, Dean Burch, that the chairman really worked for the White House and said it was a "fiction" that the FCC is "an arm of Congress." The chairman responded, "I don't want to be smart, but I've noticed on my visits to the Hill that if I say something they like, I'm an 'arm of Congress.' Otherwise, I'm an appointee of the administration." [62] Commissioners are political appointees, often with a history of party service. Some staff appointments require political clearance. It would be naive to believe that issues of political fairness do not create heavy pressures on an agency appointed by politicians. The director of President Nixon's Office of Telecommunications Policy has acknowledged that the FCC's interpretation of its fairness policy toward presidential television has produced "an intricate, confusing and inherently arbitrary series of rulings." [63] FCC rulings may actually have reduced the time allotted to the political opposition. Certainly, the FCC's decision that CBS's "Loyal Opposition" required time for a response by the presidential party did not increase the likelihood that the series would continue. The president of the Public Broadcasting Service, Hartford Gunn, Jr., believes that the complexities of the fairness doctrine, together with the administrative burden on a broadcaster policing his own "fairness," could eliminate most political programs. [64]

No other board, commission, or committee is likely to perform better than the FCC. There is much wisdom in the warning that "men of politics cannot be trusted to regulate the press, because the press deals with politics." [65] The duty of policing political broadcast fairness has forced the FCC to adopt totally unworkable guidelines. It seeks to decide fairness by analyzing broadcast content and form. It once counted lines in a script to determine if "balance" had been achieved; [66] it has found a ratio of eight cigarette ads to one antismoking spot sufficient for balance; [67] it has found that five unanswered presidential appearances can create an imbalance, but has not suggested that four, three, or two can do the same. The need for such judgments in the political area by the FCC or anyone else should be eliminated; opposition party television access should be deregulated. Instead, the national committee of the opposition party should be given by law an automatic right of response to any presidential radio or television appearance made during the ten months preceding a presidential election or within the ninety days preceding a congressional election in nonpresidential years. Section 315 of the Communications Act of 1934—the equal time provision—should be amended to provide that every radio or television broadcaster or CATV system that carries an appearance of the president within that response period must, upon request, provide equal broadcast opportunities to the national committee of the political party whose nominee for president received the second-highest number of popular votes in the most recent election for that office. Only those presidential appearances in documentaries or newscasts in which the president's appearance is only incidental, and appearances that already give rise to "equal time" for an opposition candidate, should be exempt from this requirement. (Draft legislation to accomplish these changes appears in Appendix B.)

"Equal broadcast opportunities" would mean free time when the president's time has been free, at an equally desirable time of day in terms of potential audience (for example, prime time if the president has appeared in prime time), and of a duration not necessarily identical but approximately equal to the length of the president's broadcast. The national committee should control format of the presentation if the president has had control of his format; if he has chosen a news conference, the national committee might wish to use the same format, an address, or a panel discussion. In exercising its "right of response," the party's national committee would not be limited to addressing only those issues raised by the president in his appearance. It could, for example, introduce its leaders or the party candidate or candidates in the coming election, or both.

When a presidential appearance has been carried simultaneously by the networks, the national committee response should also be carried simultaneously by the networks. Otherwise, the television exposure clearly could not be termed "equal." It has been suggested that presidential addresses be rotated among the networks, each taking a turn at carrying the address while the others advertise the address. Similarly, it has been suggested that one or all networks might delay a presidential appearance —tape the live appearance for broadcast at a later hour. This decision is best left to network judgment. If presidential simultaneity is abandoned, the party response need not be carried simultaneously.

Under this proposal, if the president delivered a prime-time, three-network broadcast address within the response period to propose an international agreement, for example, radio and television stations (and CATV systems) that carried the address would be obligated to provide the national committee of the major opposition party "equal opportunities." The only exception, since the event clearly is not a documentary or newscast in which the president's appearance is but incidental, would be if the broadcast already created a right to "equal time" for an opposition party candidate (as, for example, if it were a presidential election year, the president was a nominee, and the appearance was not within the "news" exemption of the law). Since the president had chosen the format by choosing to deliver an address instead of holding a press conference or a "conversation," the opposition party national committee would have control over the format of its presentation also. Networks and stations that carried the president simultaneously would have to carry the party simultaneously.

The party response time should be put in the hands of the party's national committee because the committee is responsible for the party's election campaign. In choosing the Democratic National Committee to speak for the opposition party in its "Loyal Opposition" series, the CBS network stated:

> The Committee does represent the party as a whole. Every state has representatives on it and a voice in its procedures and decisions. The Chairman speaks from a position organizationally representing the whole party. He and the National Committee, theoretically at least, are interim custodians of the party platform—the only set of principles and priorities formally adopted by the entire party. Finally, the National Committee and its Chairman are ordinarily the last remaining political agencies readily available for consultation to the losing candidate for the Presidency.[68]

If party members are dissatisfied with their national committee's response, they could change it. The committee surely would be more responsive to pressures from party members than would the networks.

The purpose of response time in the periods prior to federal elections is to insure equality in the electoral use of television. Each presidential television appearance can help create a favorable image of the president or his party and may change votes. Even when the president is not a candidate for reelection, his appearance can affect the candidacies of other nominees of his party.

By limiting the response period, this proposal avoids the danger, on the one hand, of over-politicizing the presidency and, on the other hand, of boring the public. If the response period were unlimited, the president might have difficulty in maintaining a consensus with which to govern; and the public would have no respite from politics. The proposal establishes the right of response during all of a presidential year before the election because in every presidential year, presidential politics begins to saturate the country even before the first primary is held, and anything a president says in the spring may strongly affect how people vote that fall. In off-years, when congressional elections are held, his influence is largely confined to the fall campaign months—the country pays little heed to congressional elections until then. And in odd-numbered years, when no federal election is held, the president need not be hampered by televised opposition but should be free to govern. The Republican National Committee has argued that "the President . . . cannot normally engage in wide-open and robust debate in fulfilling his Constitutional role as President." [69] This has merit —but it must not stultify the opposition.

In some cases, a presidential appearance during the response period might be essentially nonpolitical. Some would object that a Republican response to President Kennedy's 1962 Cuban missile crisis speech, on the eve of the congressional election, would not have served the national interest. But the opposition party is unlikely to use its right of response in its own unenlightened self-interest. That is, during a genuine crisis the public would be aware of the peril, and no politician would dare play politics with it. The opposition would not be required to respond if it did not wish to do so. In a period of national crisis the party might simply forego the time. It might even call for national unity in support of the government, explicitly subordinating partisan goals to the national interest. It would have been bad politics for the Republicans to have criticized President Kennedy during the missile crisis. And a president who claimed such a peril when none in fact existed would risk his entire position. Any presidential appearance on television in an election year has a political impact, and the opposition should have the opportunity to counter this impact under more or less equal conditions. [70]

The opposition response should be exempt from the equal time law and the fairness and political party doctrines. This is necessary to prevent a continuing "response" to a "response"

—an unnecessary and unfair burden on the broadcaster. If every side of each issue treated in these broadcasts had to be presented in some other broadcast, the rebuttals and counter rebuttals would be almost endless and might vitiate the initial opposition response. Since the purpose of the response is to equalize the electoral use of broadcasting between the president and the opposition, to give the president's party an opportunity to respond to the response would be self-defeating. Minor party response would diminish the impact of the major opposition response. While excluding minor parties here, we have tried to provide for them later on.

Between elections, the national committee of the opposition party, the national committee of the president's party, and the commercial and public television networks should together develop a plan to present live debates—perhaps titled "The National Debates"—between spokesmen for the two major parties with agreed topics and formats quarterly each year (only twice a year in federal election years). All debates should be scheduled during prime time and broadcast simultaneously by all networks. They should be widely advertised and promoted by the broadcasters and the parties. This proposal should be carried out voluntarily by the parties and networks rather than be required by legislation.

The debate format might help overcome the public's lack of interest in political programs. The Kennedy-Nixon "Great Debates" of 1960, the last nationally televised political debates between candidates, drew large audiences. The networks benefit from large audiences and take pride in their journalism; they would be likely to make every effort to present interesting programs. The national committees of the parties, too, would want to present their most arresting personalities and best debaters. The network-party combination might well produce a political program that could attract, inform, and hold a television audience.

In a similar manner, French television presents each week a program entitled "Aux Armes Egales" featuring a debate between opposing politicians. The debaters may each present a film on the subject of the debate to emphasize their arguments. Debates are presented before a live audience and the audience is given an opportunity to ask questions of either side.

Our proposal of a response right is directed at electoral equality; our proposal of national debates is intended to encourage the development of party positions. Such debates would encourage the parties to engage in serious discussions of issues to develop party positions through discussion within their own ranks, and to select spokesmen regularly—and thus to develop party leadership between elections. This process might ultimately make the parties more responsive to changes in public opinion and hence more attractive as channels for dissent than they are now.

In addition to providing television access for the opposition party, "The National Debates" would prevent unfairness to the president's party. Ordinarily, any position that the party in power takes is consistent with the president's position. But important differences sometimes arise between the president and a significant faction of his own party. President Johnson differed from a number of Democratic "doves" on Vietnam; President Nixon has been at odds with important Republican factions on Supreme Court nominations and China policy. On "The National Debates," the president's party would have an opportunity to oppose his policies if it wished.

Minor parties could also participate in "The National Debates," presenting minority viewpoints. Their participation could follow the guidelines set forth in *Voters' Time,* the 1969 report of the nonpartisan Commission on Campaign Costs in the Electronic Era, sponsored by The Twentieth Century Fund. Their participation could be made to depend upon the *Voters' Time* tests of size and vote-getting strength (these are set out in

Appendix C). A third party might be added to two of the four debates and a fourth party to one.

"The National Debates" scheme would be voluntary. It would be not only unwise but unconstitutional to require anyone by law to appear on television in a particular manner. Surely the major and minor opposition parties would need no urging to participate in "The National Debates." While some hesitancy might be anticipated from the party in power, public pressure would probably prevent it from foiling the debates. The networks perhaps could be specifically required by law or regulation to make time available for national debates, but we believe that the public-interest standard under which broadcasters hold their licenses is broad enough to include this requirement.

To remove every possible impediment to network participation, "The National Debates" should be made an exception to the "equal time" requirement of Section 315 (the draft legislation in Appendix B contains provisions to establish this exemption). In addition, the FCC should exempt the debates from fairness doctrine or political party doctrine consequences. The debates should not obligate the networks to present additional viewpoints on issues raised in the programs, nor should the debates be deemed to rectify any preexisting imbalance in the presentation of issues.

We also propose adopting *Voters' Time* reforms themselves to ensure all significant presidential candidates a minimum amount of free, simultaneous television time. The *Voters' Time* report concluded that the voters' ability to watch and assess candidates for president and vice president was in danger of being limited by the high cost of television. The report proposed therefore that each presidential candidate and his running mate be given campaign "voters' time" without cost to them—broadcast time provided simultaneously by all television and radio stations. The two major party candidates would receive six thirty-minute, prime-time program periods in the thirty-five days preceding a presidential election; candidates of minor parties of sufficient size would receive one or two half-hour periods depending on the party's relative strength. (See Appendix C for specific details of the proposal.) Candidates could use their voters' time only in formats that "promote rational political discussion and substantially involve live appearance by the candidate." The federal government would compensate broadcasters for voters' time at reduced commercial rates. Voters' time broadcasts and other appearances of presidential candidates would be exempt from the equal time law (in order to prevent very minor party candidates from claiming time). These proposals should be adopted; legislation to carry them out is set forth in Appendix C.[71] Voters' time would prevent candidates from being barred from television by lack of money, provide more time for the opposition, and elevate the campaign dialogue.

In combination, these reforms would do much to protect the traditional functions of the loyal opposition in an electronic era. During campaigns, the opposition party would have a reasonable chance to match the television influence of the incumbent president and his party. Between elections, the opposition could develop and present through debate its positions on issues. In each case, the opposition's television time would equal the president's—free, prime-time, and on all networks simultaneously. The proposals would not, and should not, guarantee successful opposition to the president. But they would provide the opposition party with what it requires to continue as a vital institution, a reasonable chance to take its case to today's marketplace of ideas—television.

CHAPTER 6

THE FUTURE
OF THE FORUM

To LEAD, a president must communicate effectively. Max Lerner has observed that to perform the enormous tasks of his office, a president must become a "Communicator-In-Chief, a function only a little lower on the scale than Commander-In-Chief and chief decision-maker in global policy."[1] Without easy access to public opinion, his leadership effectiveness is reduced. In his study of the presidency, Richard Neustadt concluded that without public opinion, a president "may not be left helpless, but his options are reduced, his opportunities diminished, his freedom for maneuver checked. . . ."[2] Even the Democratic National Committee, proponent of the right to respond to presidential television, has acknowledged that "the President's ability to communicate with, and thereby lead and govern the nation" should remain undisturbed.[3] The Republicans, too, have supported unlimited presidential television.[4]

Few would have the president communicate less. No one could seriously suggest that the nation would have been better off without FDR's "fireside chats" during a depression and a world war, Eisenhower's televised addresses after his illnesses, Kennedy's televised explanation of the Cuban blockade, Johnson's televised explanation of events in the Dominican Republic, President Nixon's many televised explanations of Vietnam policy. Those appearances did much to create an informed public. As Frank Stanton of CBS has said, "No one can complain because the elected leader of the nation has direct and unfiltered access to those to whom he is ultimately responsible. It is, in fact, one of the great triumphs of the broadcast media that they have made this possible." [5]

Because of television, the president now is *expected* to communicate regularly with the public. Because he has such easy access to a mass audience, a failure by the president to address that audience with reasonable frequency can create distrust, unease, incredibility. Television is an inescapable part of the highest public office. As one presidential adviser has observed, television "is something he is supposed to do." [6]

The problem, however, is that television is also something that the opposition political party and the Congress were "supposed to do" if they are to perform their institutional roles of checking presidential power. The president's preeminent television presence is of concern when it threatens to become a practical monopoly. The opposition party must communicate too. So must Congress. Even the Supreme Court may some day want to.

Stanton has warned:

If the words and views of the President become a monolithic force, if they constitute not just the most powerful voice in the land but the only one speaking for a nationwide point of view, then the delicate mechanism through which an enlightened public opinion is distilled . . . is thrown dangerously off balance.

Public opinion becomes not informed but instructed, and not enlightened but dominated.[7]

The proposed reforms discussed in Chapters 4 and 5 are designed to prevent that from happening. They would guarantee the opposition party and Congress a right to rebut the president on television. In summary, these reforms are:

CONGRESS: *Congress, in consultation with the television networks, should permit television cameras on the floor of the House and Senate for the broadcast of specially scheduled prime-time evening sessions at which the most important matters before it each term are discussed, debated, and voted on. The sessions should be scheduled and broadcast at least four times per year and carried simultaneously by all three networks. These broadcasts should be exempt from the "equal time" law and the fairness and political party doctrines.*

THE OPPOSITION PARTY: (1) Response Time: *Presidential television and opposition party television should be de-regulated—taken out of the hands of the FCC. The national committee of the opposition party should be given by law an automatic right of response to any presidential radio or television address made during the ten months preceding a presidential election or within the ninety days preceding a congressional election in nonpresidential years. Section 315 of the Communications Act of 1934—the equal time provision—should be amended to provide that every radio or television broadcaster or CATV system that carries an address of the president within that response period must, upon request, provide equal broadcast opportunities to the national committee of the political party whose nominee for president has received the second-highest number of popular votes in the most recent election for that office. Only those presidential appearances in documentaries or newscasts in which the president's appearance is* *only incidental, and appearances which already give rise to "equal time" for an opposition candidate, should be exempt from this requirement. "Equal broadcast opportunities" would mean free time when the president's time has been free, at an equally desirable time of day in terms of potential audience (for example, prime time if the president has appeared in prime time). The national committee should control format if the president has had control of his format. The national committee would not be limited to addressing only those issues raised by the president in his appearance. When a presidential appearance has been carried simultaneously by all three networks, the national committee response should also be carried simultaneously by the networks. The national committee should choose its spokesman or spokesmen. The opposition response should be exempt from the "equal time" law and the fairness and political party doctrines.*

*(2) **National Debates:** Between elections, the national committee of the opposition party, the national committee of the president's party, and the commercial and public television networks should together develop a plan to present live debates— "The National Debates"—between spokesmen for the two major parties with agreed topics and formats quarterly each year (but only twice in federal election years). All debates should be scheduled during prime time and broadcast simultaneously by all networks. This proposal should be carried out voluntarily by the parties and networks rather than be required by legislation. Minor parties would participate in "The National Debates" according to the guidelines set forth in* Voters' Time *(the 1969 report of the nonpartisan Commission on Campaign Costs in the Electronic Era, sponsored by The Twentieth Century Fund, Inc.). "The National Debates" should be exempt from the "equal time" law and the fairness and political party doctrines.*

*(3) **Voters' Time:** The reforms proposed in* Voters' Time

should be adopted to ensure all significant presidential candi-
dates a minimum amount of free, simultaneous television time.
The two major party candidates would receive six thirty-minute
prime-time program periods in the thirty-five days preceding a
presidential election; candidates of minor parties of sufficient
size (based on a formula contained in the Voters' Time *report)*
would receive one or two half-hour periods depending on their
party's relative strength.

THE SUPREME COURT: *Various steps should be taken to*
improve the coverage of the Court's decisions, but the justices
of the Court should remain outside the television spotlight (see
Chapter 3).

OTHER PARTIES: *See next paragraph.*

These reforms, taken together, should redress the balance now
heavily tilted toward the president. But in the world of politics
and government the unexpected regularly occurs. In such circumstances, balance can evaporate and the public's right to
receive differing views or to gauge the personality of all significant candidates can be impeded despite the balancing mechanism. It is not always the party or the Congress that can speak
for the opposition. To allow for the unexpected and to add flexi-
bility, responsible spokesmen of any kind should not be pre-
vented from purchasing a reasonable amount of time. Broadcasters should set aside a portion of commercial advertising
time for purchase by responsible spokesmen on a first-come,
first-served basis. This would enable the opposition party, a
minor party, or members of Congress to buy additional time.
Even the Supreme Court, in its recent DNC decision, left the
door open for such reform: "Conceivably at some future date
Congress or the [FCC]—or the broadcasters—may devise some
kind of limited right of access that is both practicable and
desirable." Moreover, such groups as Common Cause, which
believe that neither the political parties nor Congress always

oppose the president strenuously enough, would have somewhat greater access to television.[8]

If all of the suggested reform steps are taken, any issue discussed during a presidential television appearance could also be discussed on television by the opposition party and its candidates, minor party candidates, members of Congress, and anyone wishing to purchase broadcast time. As a result, the continued application to presidential television of the "fairness doctrine," "political party doctrine," or any other regulatory theory involving discretionary administrative "balancing" would be unnecessary. As long as they present the opportunity, fairness and similar doctrines would continue to be used as a basis for complaints from politicians, members of Congress, and others that issues discussed by the president require even more balancing than would be provided if all these reforms were adopted. But, because the reforms would provide reasonable opportunity for the discussion of issues and the cultivation of images, the long FCC and court proceedings that seem to have become a trademark of existing fairness regulation in this area would be unnecessary, thus conserving the energies of all concerned. No one is likely to gain television access by way of a fairness complaint at the FCC who could not more easily gain reasonable access through one of the reforms described here. A presidential radio or television appearance, therefore, should have no regulatory consequences beyond those specified in the reforms proposed in Chapters 4 and 5.

Reforms today may not suffice for tomorrow. The beginning of national radio is recent enough to be within the memory of most adult people; the beginning of mass visual communication by television is remembered by many people. There is no reason to believe that an area so new will go unchanged. The future of television and other media as a forum for political debate will present new capabilities and new problems. Future presidents will experiment with new, innovative formats. We may see televised discussions between the president and international leaders, regularly scheduled presidential reports to the nation, presidential "spots" of one minute or less.

In years to come, presidents will experiment with visual aids in presenting their viewpoints on television. President Kennedy used maps to illustrate some of his televised remarks; President Nixon has employed both film clips and charts. Presidents in the 1970s and 1980s may be expected to try other techniques, such as longer films or on-location settings. It is not likely that future presidents will be content to sit in front of a television camera reading a speech from a text held in their hands or from a teleprompter.

Rapidly approaching technology will add new dimensions to presidential television. The recent growth of cable television means greatly expanded television choices. Cable subscribers receive programs and information through a cable rather than by an antenna that picks up signals in the air. Instead of the limited number of over-the-air channels, cable television gives the viewer a choice among up to forty separate channels. Cable subscribers will receive not only programs from local television stations but also programs delivered directly to them by cable. This already is leading to community and regional channels that can beam programs at special interest groups. A future president, instead of always addressing the whole country, will aim taped reports directly at racial, regional, economic, or ethnic minorities.

Cable television also makes feasible a national government information channel. It might provide information about social security benefits, home loans, or other government programs. It could make it possible to file a tax return, apply for veteran's benefits, or vote direct from the home. Such a channel might alarm many people, who might fear its perversion into an administration propaganda machine. New developments, however, bring with them new issues. An entire cable channel could be devoted solely to politics, including party programs, sessions of Congress, and congressional committee hearings. Over the cable, a congressman could speak only to his constituents, as he cannot now. In the more distant future, viewers could talk back to their television sets by cable, responding to a poll by their senator or a question by their president. Cable television could put elected officials in constant touch with their constituency.

Other technological developments can be expected. A number of companies already produce videocassettes and videocassette players and recorders—visual versions of the popular cassette stereo tapes and players. In the next decade, these devices will become inexpensive. Political parties can produce videotape programs and circulate them to homes and local meetings. Congressional hearings and debates could be videotaped.

Ben Bagdikian, formerly of the *Washington Post,* writes that coming changes in communication technology "will be to politics what nuclear fission was to physical weapons, an increase in power so great that it constitutes a new condition for mankind." [9] Television, virtually unknown thirty years ago, today has the power to capture the simultaneous attention of nearly the entire American population. Bagdikian says the "new communications will permit the accumulation of a critical mass of human attention and impulse that up to now has been inconceivable." It is none too soon to begin public discussion of the issues raised by developing technology.

Meanwhile, the problems of presidential television as it exists today must be solved. At present, the president enjoys an overwhelming communications advantage over the opposition party and the Congress. That balance must be redressed. It is time—it is far past time—to adopt reforms that will help television create a true national town meeting, capable of fully informing a free people on the issues and choices before them.

APPENDIXES

APPENDIX A
Tables

169

TABLE 1

Television Use by Presidents Nixon, Johnson, and Kennedy during First Nineteen Months in Office

	Nixon	Johnson	Kennedy
Number of appearances in prime time	14	7	4
Length of time on air in prime time (hours)	7.05	3.33	1.9
Total number of appearances	37	33	50
Total length of time on air (hours)	13.5	12.5	30.25

Source: figures supplied by the White House Press Office, quoted in the *New York Times,* August 3, 1970, p. 16. Computation includes only speeches and press conferences carried live on national television networks.

TABLE 2

Broadcasts Made by President Nixon on Radio Only
January 20, 1969–April 30, 1972

Date	Time *	Subject
Oct. 17, 1969	4:00 P.M.	Rising cost of living
Feb. 25, 1971	11:00 A.M.	Foreign policy
Apr. 16, 1971	9:00 P.M.	Question-and-answer session with American Society of Newspaper Editors
May 1, 1971	1:00 P.M.	News conference
May 2, 1971	3:00 P.M.	Salute to agriculture
May 7, 1971	10:00 A.M.	Salute to agriculture
Sept. 6, 1971	12:00 M.	Labor Day
Sept. 23, 1971	9:00 P.M.	Question-and-answer session at Economic Club of Detroit
Oct. 24, 1971	7:30 P.M.	Veterans Day
Feb. 9, 1972	11:05 A.M.	Foreign policy

* Eastern Standard Time.

TABLE 3

President Nixon's Radio and Television News Conferences

January 20, 1969–April 30, 1972

Date *	Time **
Jan. 27, 1969	11:00 A.M.
Feb. 6, 1969	11:00 A.M.
Mar. 4, 1969	9:00 P.M.
Mar. 14, 1969	12:00 M.
Apr. 18, 1969	11:30 A.M.
June 19, 1969	7:00 P.M.
Sept. 26, 1969	12:00 M.
Dec. 8, 1969	9:00 P.M.
Jan. 30, 1970	6:30 P.M.
May 8, 1970	10:00 P.M.
July 30, 1970	11:00 P.M. (broadcast from Calif.)
Dec. 10, 1970	7:00 P.M.
Mar. 4, 1971	9:00 P.M.
Apr. 29, 1971	9:00 P.M.
May 1, 1971	1:00 P.M. (radio only)
June 1, 1971	8:30 P.M.

* All broadcasts were carried live on ABC, CBS, and NBC.
** Eastern Standard Time.

TABLE 4

Network Television Addresses by President Nixon
January 20, 1969–April 30, 1972

Date *	Time **	Subject
May 14, 1969	10:00 P.M.	Southeast Asia: Vietnam
Aug. 8, 1969	10:00 P.M.	Domestic programs: Welfare system over-haul
Nov. 3, 1969	9:30 P.M.	Southeast Asia: Vietnamization announced
Dec. 15, 1969	6:00 P.M.	Southeast Asia: Progress toward peace
Jan. 26, 1970	9:00 P.M.	Veto of HEW appropriations bill
Mar. 23, 1970	2:15 P.M.	Postal strike: Emergency declared
Apr. 20, 1970	9:00 P.M.	Southeast Asia: Vietnam
Apr. 30, 1970	9:00 P.M.	Southeast Asia: Cambodian invasion
June 3, 1970	9:00 P.M.	Southeast Asia: Cambodian sanctuary operation
June 17, 1970	12:00 M.	Economic policy and productivity
Oct. 7, 1970	9:00 P.M.	Southeast Asia: New peace initiative
Apr. 7, 1971	9:00 P.M.	Southeast Asia: Vietnam
May 20, 1971	12:00 M.	Strategic Arms Limitation Talks (SALT) agreement with USSR
July 15, 1971	10:30 P.M.	Announcement of trip to the People's Republic of China
Aug. 15, 1971	9:00 P.M.	The Economy: The new prosperity
Oct. 7, 1971	7:30 P.M.	The Economy: Phase II
Jan. 25, 1972	8:30 P.M.	Southeast Asia: Indochina peace proposal
Mar. 16, 1972	10:00 P.M.	Domestic issues: Busing
Apr. 26, 1972	10:00 P.M.	Southeast Asia: Vietnam

* All addresses were carried live on ABC, CBS, and NBC and preempted regular programming.
** Eastern Standard Time.

TABLE 5

Network Television Appearances of President Nixon on Special News Programs

January 20, 1969–April 30, 1972

Date	Time*	Subject	Program Format	Network Coverage
Jan. 20, 1969	All day	Inaugural ceremonies	Network news special	ABC, CBS, NBC (live)
May 21, 1969	7:00 P.M.	Nomination of Warren Burger as Chief Justice of the Supreme Court	Network news special	ABC, CBS, NBC (live)
June 4, 1969	11:30 A.M.	Air Force Academy speech	Network news special	ABC, CBS, NBC (live)
Sept. 18, 1969	11:20 A.M.	UN address	Network news special	ABC, CBS, NBC (live)
Jan. 22, 1970	12:30 P.M.	State of the Union	Network news special	ABC, CBS, NBC (live)
July 1, 1970	10:00 P.M.	Foreign policy	Conversation / interview	ABC, CBS, NBC (live)
Sept. 16, 1970	1:00 P.M.	Speech at Kansas State University	Network news special	ABC, CBS, NBC (live)
Oct. 23, 1970	4:00 P.M.	Speech at UN General Assembly	Network news special	ABC, CBS, NBC (live)
Jan. 4, 1971	9:00 P.M.		Conversation / interview with four network correspondents	ABC, CBS, NBC PBS (live)
Jan. 22, 1971	9:00 P.M.	State of the Union	Network news special	ABC, CBS, NBC, PBS (live)
Mar. 17, 1971	11:30 A.M.	Eulogy for Whitney Young	Ceremonial / news	ABC, CBS, NBC (live)

Date	Time*	Event		Networks
Mar. 22, 1971	9:30 P.M.		Conversation/interview with Howard K. Smith	ABC (live)
May 22, 1971	1:00 P.M.	Lyndon B. Johnson Library dedication	Ceremonial/news	ABC, CBS, NBC (live)
Sept. 9, 1971	12:30 P.M.	Special address to Congress on the new economic policy	Network news special	ABC, CBS, NBC (live)
Oct. 21, 1971	7:30 P.M.	Supreme Court nominations	Network news special	ABC, CBS, NBC (live), PBS (delayed)
Jan. 2, 1972	9:30 P.M.		Conversation/interview with Dan Rather	CBS (live)
Jan. 20, 1972	12:30 P.M.	State of the Union	Network news special	ABC, CBS, NBC, PBS (live)
Feb. 17–28, 1972		Trip to the People's Republic of China	Network news specials	ABC, CBS, NBC, PBS (live and film)

* Eastern Standard Time.

TABLE 6

Miscellaneous Television Appearances of President Nixon
January 20, 1969–April 30, 1972

Date	Time*	Subject	Program Format	Network Coverage
July 20, 1969	12:00 P.M.	Phone call to Apollo 11 astronauts	Network news special	ABC, CBS, NBC (live)
July 24, 1969	11:30 A.M.–2:45 P.M.	Apollo 11 splashdown	Network news special	ABC, CBS, NBC (live)
Nov. 5, 1969	8:30 A.M.	Texas–Arkansas football game	Informal interview	NBC (live)
Dec. 6, 1969	2:40 P.M.			ABC (live)
Dec. 16, 1969	5:30 P.M.	Christmas tree lighting	Ceremonial / news	ABC, CBS, NBC (live)
Aug. 31, 1970	8:00 A.M.		Interview	CBS (tape)
Oct. 30, 1970	11:30 P.M.	Anaheim campaign speech	Paid political broadcast (paid for by RNC)	CBS (tape)
Nov. 2, 1970		Phoenix campaign speech	Paid political broadcast (paid for by RNC)	ABC, CBS, NBC (tape)

Date	Time	Event	Category	Network
Dec. 16, 1970	5:30 P.M.	Christmas tree lighting	Ceremonial / news	ABC, CBS, NBC (live)
Mar. 15, 1971	7:00 A.M.	Wedding of Tricia Nixon and Edward Cox	Informal interview	NBC (tape)
June 12, 1971	6:00 P.M. (CBS, 60 min.) 6:00 P.M. (NBC, 30 min.) 7:00 P.M. (ABC, 30 min.) 7:30 P.M. (NBC, 60 min.)		Ceremonial / news	ABC, CBS, NBC (tape)
July 3, 1971	10:30 P.M.	American Revolution Bicentennial Era	Ceremonial / news	ABC, CBS, NBC (live)
July 31, 1971	Approximately 6:00 P.M.	Professional Football Hall of Fame game	Interview with sportscaster Frank Gifford	ABC (tape)
Dec. 21, 1971	7:30 P.M.	A Day in the Presidency	Documentary / news	NBC (tape)

* Eastern Standard Time.

177

TABLE 7
Network Television and Radio Broadcasts of President Nixon
January 20, 1969–April 30, 1972

Interval since Last Television Appearance	Date of Broadcast	Time *	Subject	Program Format **
	Jan. 20, 1969	All day	Inaugural ceremonies	News special
1 week	Jan. 27, 1969	11:00 A.M.		News conference
1½ weeks	Feb. 6, 1969	11:00 A.M.		News conference
3½ weeks	Mar. 4, 1969	9:00 P.M.		News conference
1½ weeks	Mar. 14, 1969	12:00 M.		News conference
5 weeks	Apr. 18, 1969	11:30 A.M.		News conference
3½ weeks	May 14, 1969	10:00 P.M.	Southeast Asia: Vietnam	Address (preemption)
1 week	May 21, 1969	7:00 P.M.	Nomination of Warren Burger as Chief Justice of the Supreme Court	News special
2 weeks	June 4, 1969	11:30 A.M.	Air Force Academy speech	News special
2 weeks	June 19, 1969	7:00 P.M.		News conference
4½ weeks	July 20, 1969	12:00 P.M.	Phone call to Apollo 11 astronauts	News special
½ week	July 24, 1969	11:30 A.M.	Apollo 11 splashdown	News special

2 weeks	Aug. 8, 1969	10:00 P.M.	Domestic programs: Welfare system overhaul	Address (preemption)
7 weeks	Sept. 18, 1969	11:20 A.M.	UN address	News special
1 week	Sept. 26, 1969	12:00 M.		News conference
7½ weeks	Oct. 17, 1969	4:00 P.M.	Rising cost of living	Address (preemption; radio only)
½ week	Nov. 3, 1969	9:30 P.M.	Southeast Asia: Vietnamization	Address (preemption)
	Nov. 5, 1969	8:30 A.M.		Interview (NBC only)
4½ weeks	Dec. 6, 1969	2:40 P.M.	Texas-Arkansas football game	Interview (ABC only)
½ week	Dec. 8, 1969	9:00 P.M.		News conference
1 week	Dec. 15, 1969	6:00 P.M.	Southeast Asia: Progress toward peace	Address (preemption)
1 day	Dec. 16, 1969	5:30 P.M.	Christmas tree lighting	News special
5½ weeks	Jan. 22, 1970	12:30 P.M.	State of the Union	News special
½ week	Jan. 26, 1970	9:00 P.M.	Veto of HEW appropriations bill	Address (preemption)
½ week	Jan. 30, 1970	6:30 P.M.		News conference
7½ weeks	Mar. 23, 1970	2:15 P.M.	Postal strike: Emergency declared	Address (preemption)
4 weeks	Apr. 20, 1970	9:00 P.M.	Southeast Asia: Vietnam	Address (preemption)
1½ weeks	Apr. 30, 1970	9:00 P.M.	Southeast Asia: Cambodian invasion	Address (preemption)

TABLE 7 (*Continued*)

Network Television and Radio Broadcasts of President Nixon
January 20, 1969–April 30, 1972

Interval since Last Television Appearance	Date of Broadcast	Time *	Subject	Program Format
1 week	May 8, 1970	10:00 P.M.	Southeast Asia: Cambodian sanctuary operation	News conference
4 weeks	June 3, 1970	9:00 P.M.		Address (preemption)
2 weeks	June 17, 1970	12:00 M.	Economic policy and productivity	Address (preemption)
2 weeks	July 1, 1970	10:00 P.M.	Foreign policy	Conversation/interview
4 weeks	July 30, 1970	11:00 P.M.		News conference
4½ weeks	Aug. 31, 1970	8:00 A.M.		Interview (CBS only; tape)
2½ weeks	Sept. 16, 1970	1:00 P.M.	Speech at Kansas State University	News special
3 weeks	Oct. 7, 1970	9:00 P.M.	Southeast Asia: New peace initiative	Address (preemption)
2 weeks	Oct. 23, 1970	4:00 P.M.	Speech at UN General Assembly	News special
1 week	Oct. 30, 1970	11:30 P.M.	Anaheim campaign speech	Paid political broadcast (CBS only; tape)
3 days	Nov. 2, 1970	8:30 P.M.	Phoenix campaign speech	Paid political broadcast
6 weeks	Dec. 10, 1970	7:00 P.M.		News conference
1 week	Dec. 16, 1970	5:30 P.M.	Christmas tree lighting	News special

3 weeks	Jan. 4, 1971	9:00 P.M.		Conversation/interview
2½ weeks	Jan. 22, 1971	9:00 P.M.	State of the Union	News special
	Feb. 25, 1971	11:00 A.M.	Foreign policy	Address (preemption; radio only)
6 weeks	Mar. 4, 1971	9:00 P.M.		News conference
1½ weeks	Mar. 15, 1971	7:00 A.M.		Interview (NBC only; tape)
½ week	Mar. 17, 1971	11:30 A.M.	Eulogy for Whitney Young	News special
½ week	Mar. 22, 1971	9:30 P.M.		Conversation/interview with Howard K. Smith (ABC only)
2½ weeks	Apr. 7, 1971	9:00 P.M.	Southeast Asia: Vietnam	Address (preemption)
	Apr. 16, 1971	9:00 P.M.	Question-and-answer session with American Society of Newspaper Editors	News special (radio only)
3 weeks	Apr. 29, 1971	9:00 P.M.		News conference
	May 1, 1971	1:00 P.M.		News conference (radio only)
	May 2, 1971	3:00 P.M.	Salute to agriculture	News special (radio only)
	May 7, 1971	10:00 A.M.	Salute to agriculture	News special (radio only)
3 weeks	May 20, 1971	12:00 M.	SALT agreement with USSR	Address (preemption)
2 days	May 22, 1971	1:00 P.M.	LBJ Library dedication	News special
1½ weeks	June 1, 1971	8:30 P.M.		News conference
1½ weeks	June 12, 1971	6:00 P.M. (CBS) 6:00 P.M. (NBC) 7:00 P.M. (ABC) 7:30 P.M. (NBC)	Nixon-Cox wedding	News special

TABLE 7 (*Continued*)

Network Television and Radio Broadcasts of President Nixon

January 20, 1969–April 30, 1972

Interval since Last Television Appearance	Date of Broadcast	Time *	Subject	Program Format **
3 weeks	July 3, 1971	10:30 P.M.	American Revolution Bicentennial Era	News special
1½ weeks	July 15, 1971	10:30 P.M.	Trip to the People's Republic of China	News special (preemption)
2½ weeks	July 31, 1971	Approximately 6:00 P.M.	Football	Interview with sportscaster Frank Gifford (ABC only)
2 weeks	Aug. 15, 1971	9:00 P.M.	The Economy: The new prosperity	Address (preemption)
3 weeks	Sept. 6, 1971	12:00 M.	Labor Day	Address (preemption; radio only)
½ week	Sept. 9, 1971	12:30 P.M.	The Economy	News special
2 weeks	Sept. 23, 1971	9:00 P.M.	Question-and-answer session at Economic Club of Detroit	News special (radio only)

2 weeks	Oct. 7, 1971	7:30 P.M.	The Economy: Phase II	Address (preemption)
2 weeks	Oct. 21, 1971	7:30 P.M.	Supreme Court nominations	News special
½ week	Oct. 24, 1971	7:30 P.M.	Veterans Day	Address (preemption; radio only)
10 weeks	Jan. 2, 1972	9:30 P.M.		Conversation/interview (CBS only)
2½ weeks	Jan. 20, 1972	12:30 P.M.	State of the Union	News special
½ week	Jan. 25, 1972	8:30 P.M.	Southeast Asia: Indochina peace proposal	Address (preemption)
2 weeks	Feb. 9, 1972	11:05 A.M.	Foreign policy	Address (preemption; radio only)
1 week	Feb. 17–28, 1972		Trip to the People's Republic of China	News specials
2½ weeks	Mar. 16, 1972	10:00 P.M.	Domestic issues: Busing	Address (preemption)
6 weeks	Apr. 26, 1972	10:00 P.M.	Southeast Asia: Vietnam	Address (preemption)

* Eastern Standard Time.
** Unless otherwise indicated, all television appearances were carried live on the three major commercial networks.

T A B L E 8

Major Network Appearances of Administration Spokesmen

January 1, 1970–June 15, 1970

Date	Program	Spokesman	Program Format
Jan. 11, 1970	Face the Nation (CBS)	Melvin Laird, Sec. of Defense	Interview
Jan. 18, 1970	Issues and Answers (ABC)	William Rogers, Sec. of State	Interview
Jan. 25, 1970	Face the Nation (CBS)	Robert Finch, Sec. of HEW; Walter Hickel, Sec. of Interior; Daniel Moynihan, Counsellor to the President	Interview
Feb. 1, 1970	Face the Nation (CBS)	Vice President Spiro Agnew	Interview
Feb. 4, 1970	Today (NBC)	Maurice Stans, Sec. of Commerce	Informal interview
Feb. 5, 1970	Today (NBC)	Bryce Harlow, Counsellor to the President	Informal interview
Feb. 6, 1970	Today (NBC)	Will Wilson, Asst. Atty. Gen.	Informal interview
Feb. 8, 1970	Meet the Press (NBC)	David Kennedy, Sec. of the Treasury; Paul Mc-Cracken, Chm. of CEA; Robert Mayo, Dir. of Bur. of the Budget	Interview
Feb. 22, 1970	Meet the Press (NBC)	Melvin Laird, Sec. of Defense	Interview
Mar. 15, 1970	Issues and Answers (ABC)	Thomas Paine, Admin. of NASA	Interview
Mar. 16, 1970	Today (NBC)	Vice President Spiro Agnew	Informal interview
Mar. 17, 1970	Today (NBC)	William Rogers, Sec. of State	Informal interview
Mar. 18, 1970	Today (NBC)	George Romney, Sec. of HUD	Informal interview
Mar. 20, 1970	Today (NBC)	Rep. Rogers C. B. Morton, RNC Chm.; Sen. Hugh Scott, Senate Minority Leader	Informal interview
Mar. 22, 1970	Issues and Answers (ABC)	Sen. Hugh Scott, Senate Minority Leader	Interview
Mar. 22, 1970	Face the Nation (CBS)	Jerris Leonard, Asst. Atty. Gen.	Interview
Mar. 24, 1970	Today (NBC)	George Shultz, Sec. of Labor	Informal interview
Mar. 26, 1970	Today (NBC)	Herbert Klein, Dir. of Communications for the Exec. Branch	Informal interview

Date	Program	Person	Type
Mar. 29, 1970	Issues and Answers (ABC)	Richard Kleindienst, Dep. Atty. Gen.	Interview
Mar. 30, 1970	Today (NBC)	John Volpe, Sec. of Transportation	Informal interview
Apr. 16, 1970	Today (NBC)	Rep. Gerald Ford, House Minority Leader	Informal interview
Apr. 23, 1970	Today (NBC)	Walter Hickel, Sec. of Interior; Russell Train, Under Sec. of Interior; Thomas Williams, HEW	Informal interview
May 3, 1970	Face the Nation (CBS)	Vice President Spiro Agnew	Interview
May 10, 1970	Issues and Answers (ABC)	Elliot Richardson, Under Sec. of State	Interview
May 10, 1970	Meet the Press (NBC)	Ellsworth Bunker, Amb. to South Vietnam	Interview
May 12, 1970	Today (NBC)	Joseph Blatchford, Peace Corps Dir.	Informal interview
May 22, 1970	Today (NBC)	Melvin Laird, Sec. of Defense	Informal interview
May 24, 1970	Face the Nation (CBS)	Herbert Klein, Dir. of Communications for the Exec. Branch	Interview
May 28, 1970	Today (NBC)	Charles Walker, Under Sec. of the Treasury	Informal interview
June 3, 1970	Today (NBC)	Clark Mollenhoff, Spec. Asst. to the President	Informal interview
June 7, 1970	Face the Nation (CBS)	William Rogers, Sec. of State	Interview
June 11, 1970	Today (NBC)	Herbert Klein, Dir. of Communications for the Exec. Branch	Informal interview

This list is composed of all appearances by top administration officials and the Republican congressional leadership on "Meet the Press," "Face the Nation," "Issues and Answers," and "Today" during a representative twenty-four-week period in 1970. Sources: ABC, CBS, and NBC.

T A B L E 9

Major Television Appearances of Opposition Party Spokesmen

January 20, 1969–August 1, 1971

Date	Program	Spokesman	Program Format
Feb. 2, 1969	Issues and Answers (ABC)	Sen. Mike Mansfield, Senate Majority Leader	Interview
Feb. 23, 1969	Issues and Answers (ABC)	Rep. John McCormack, Speaker of the House	Interview
Mar. 9, 1969	Issues and Answers (ABC)	Hubert Humphrey, Democratic presidential nominee	Interview
Mar. 30, 1969	Meet the Press (NBC)	Sen. Mike Mansfield	Interview
Apr. 20, 1969	Meet the Press (NBC)	Hubert Humphrey	Interview
Apr. 27, 1969	Face the Nation (CBS)	Sen. Mike Mansfield	Interview
May 5, 1969	Today (NBC)	Hubert Humphrey	Informal interview
May 13, 1969	Today (NBC)	Hubert Humphrey	Informal interview
June 1, 1969	Issues and Answers (ABC)	Sen. Fred Harris, DNC Chm.	Interview
June 9, 1969	Mike Douglas Show (syndicated)	Sen. Fred Harris	Variety / talk show
July 6, 1969	Meet the Press (NBC)	Sen. George McGovern, Sen. Harold Hughes	Interview
July 27, 1969	Face the Nation (CBS)	Hubert Humphrey	Interview
Aug. 17, 1969	Meet the Press (NBC)	Sen. Edmund Muskie, Democratic vice-presidential nominee	Interview
Sept. 14, 1969	Issues and Answers (ABC)	Sen. Mike Mansfield	Interview
Sept. 30, 1969	Merv Griffin Show (CBS)	Sen. Edmund Muskie	Variety / talk show
Oct. 19, 1969	Issues and Answers (ABC)	Sen. Edmund Muskie	Interview
Oct. 19, 1969	Meet the Press (NBC)	Sen. Fred Harris	Informal interview
Oct. 29, 1969	Today (NBC)	Sen. Edmund Muskie	Informal interview
	Dick Cavett Show (ABC)	Sen. Fred Harris	Talk show
Nov. 18, 1969	Today (NBC)	Hubert Humphrey	Informal interview
Jan. 4, 1970	Face the Nation (CBS)	Sen. Fred Harris	Interview
Jan. 6, 1970	Today (NBC)	Sen. Mike Mansfield	Informal interview

Date	Program	Person(s)	Format
Jan. 25, 1970	Issues and Answers (ABC)	Hubert Humphrey	Interview
Jan. 28, 1970	Today (NBC)	Hubert Humphrey	Informal interview
Feb. 1, 1970	Issues and Answers (ABC)	Sen. Mike Mansfield	Interview
Feb. 1, 1970	Meet the Press (NBC)	Sen. Edmund Muskie	Interview
Feb. 8, 1970	State of the Union: A Democratic View (ABC, CBS, 1:00–2:00 P.M.; NBC, 2:30–3:30 P.M.)	12 Democratic senators, 8 Democratic congressmen	Special (produced by the Democratic Party; film)
Feb. 23, 1970	Today (NBC)	Hubert Humphrey	Informal interview
Feb. 25, 1970	Today (NBC)	Sen. Edmund Muskie	Informal interview
Mar. 3, 1970	Today (NBC)	Hubert Humphrey	Informal interview
Mar. 8, 1970	Face the Nation (CBS)	Sen. Mike Mansfield	Interview
Mar. 15, 1970	Meet the Press (NBC)	Lawrence O'Brien, DNC Chm.	Interview
Apr. 21, 1970	CBS Morning News	Sen. Edmund Muskie	Interview
Apr. 26, 1970	Issues and Answers (ABC)	Sen. Edmund Muskie	Interview
May 3, 1970	The Loyal Opposition (NBC)	Hubert Humphrey; Senators George McGovern, Adlai Stevenson III, and Abraham Ribicoff; Mayor Sam Yorty; Lawrence O'Brien	Study of Democratic Party (film and tape)
May 9, 1970	Policy address on Indochina (ABC)	Lawrence O'Brien	Network news special
May 17, 1970	Face the Nation (CBS)	Sen. Mike Mansfield	Interview
June 24, 1970	Response to Nixon address on the economy (ABC, NBC)	Sen. Mike Mansfield	Controlled by user
July 6, 1970	NOW Show: "The Loyal Opposition" (ABC, 10:30–11:00 P.M.)	Lawrence O'Brien, Sen. Edmund Muskie, Rep. Henry Reuss	Interview
July 7, 1970	The Democrats Respond: Part I (CBS, 10:00–10:30 P.M.)	Lawrence O'Brien	Controlled by user
Aug. 24, 1970	CBS Morning News (10 min.)	Lawrence O'Brien	Interview
Aug. 30, 1970	Issues and Answers (ABC)	Lawrence O'Brien	Interview

T A B L E   9 (*Continued*)

Major Television Appearances of Opposition Party Spokesmen

January 20, 1969–August 1, 1971

Date	Program	Spokesman	Program Format
Oct. 7, 1970	Politics '70 (NET, 9:30 P.M.)	Lawrence O'Brien	News special
Nov. 1, 1970	Issues and Answers (ABC)	Lawrence O'Brien *	Interview
Nov. 2, 1970	Campaign speech in response to Nixon's Phoenix campaign speech (ABC, CBS, NBC, 15 min.)	Sen. Edmund Muskie	Paid political broadcast
Nov. 5, 1970	Today (NBC)	Lawrence O'Brien	Informal interview
Nov. 22, 1970	Issues and Answers (ABC)	Senator Mike Mansfield **	Interview
Jan. 3, 1971	Issues and Answers (ABC)	Rep. John McCormack	Interview
Jan. 4, 1971	Today (NBC)	Rep. John McCormack	Informal interview
Jan. 21, 1971	Today (NBC)	Sen. George McGovern ***	Informal interview
Jan. 24, 1971	Meet the Press (NBC)	Rep. Carl Albert, Speaker of the House	Interview
Jan. 24, 1971	Face the Nation (CBS)	Sen. Mike Mansfield	Interview
Jan. 26, 1971	Merv Griffin Show (CBS)	Sen. Edmund Muskie	Variety / talk show
Jan. 26, 1971	The State of the Union: A Democratic Reply (ABC, CBS, NBC, PBS, 10:00–11:00 P.M.)	Sen. Mike Mansfield	Interview with 4 network correspondents
Jan. 28, 1971	Mike Douglas Show (syndicated)	Sen. George McGovern	Variety / talk show
Feb. 7, 1971	Issues and Answers (ABC)	Sen. Edmund Muskie	Interview
Feb. 8, 1971	David Frost Show (syndicated)	Sen. George McGovern	Talk show
Feb. 10, 1971	Mike Douglas Show (syndicated)	Sen. Hubert Humphrey	Variety / talk show
Feb. 21, 1971	Meet the Press (NBC)	Sen. George McGovern	Interview

Feb. 25, 1971	CBS Morning News	Sen. Hubert Humphrey	Interview
Feb. 28, 1971	Meet the Press (NBC)	Sen. Hubert Humphrey	Interview
Mar. 3, 1971	Today (NBC)	Sen. Hubert Humphrey	Informal interview
Mar. 21, 1971	Issues and Answers (ABC)	Sen. George McGovern	Interview
Mar. 22, 1971	Earth Day: One Year Later (CBS)	Sen. Edmund Muskie	Network news special
Mar. 28, 1971	Meet the Press (NBC)	Sen. Mike Mansfield	Interview
Mar. 31, 1971	David Frost Show (syndicated)	Sen. Edmund Muskie	Talk show
Apr. 6, 1971	Dick Cavett Show (ABC)	Sen. Hubert Humphrey	Talk show
Apr. 6, 1971	Mike Douglas Show (syndicated)	Sen. Edmund Muskie	Variety/talk show
Apr. 22, 1971	Response to Nixon's address on Southeast Asia, "Indochina: Another View" (ABC, 9:00 P.M.)	Lawrence O'Brien; Senators Jackson, Humphrey, Bayh, McGovern, Hughes, and Muskie	Controlled by user
Apr. 30, 1971	The Loyal Opposition (NBC, 10:00 P.M.)	Senators Jackson, Humphrey, Bayh, McGovern, Hughes, and Muskie	Controlled by user
May 9, 1971	Face the Nation (CBS)	Lawrence O'Brien	Interview
May 28, 1971	Today (NBC)	Sen. Hubert Humphrey	Informal interview
June 13, 1971	Issues and Answers (ABC)	Sen. Hubert Humphrey	Interview
June 20, 1971	Face the Nation (CBS)	Sen. George McGovern	Interview
July 3, 1971	American Revolution Bicentennial Era (ABC, CBS, NBC)	Rep. Carl Albert	Network news special

This list includes appearances made by Democratic National Committee spokesmen, the Senate Majority Leader, the Speaker of the House, the 1968 Democratic presidential and vice-presidential candidates, and announced candidates for the 1972 presidential nomination. Programs include the weekly interview shows ("Meet the Press," "Face the Nation," and "Issues and Answers"), the "Today" show, special network news broadcasts, and other programs listed by the press offices of the spokesmen.

    * In a one-hour special with RNC Chairman Rogers C. B. Morton.
    ** In a one-hour special with Senate Minority Leader Hugh Scott.
    *** Senator McGovern announced his candidacy for the Democratic presidential nomination on January 18, 1971.

TABLE 10
Major Television Appearances Made by Congressional Leaders
January 20, 1969–August 1, 1971

Date	Program	Spokesman	Program Format
Feb. 2, 1969	Issues and Answers (ABC)	Sen. Mike Mansfield, Senate Majority Leader	Interview
Feb. 23, 1969	Issues and Answers (ABC)	Rep. John McCormack, Speaker of the House	Interview
Mar. 30, 1969	Meet the Press (NBC)	Sen. Mike Mansfield	Interview
Apr. 27, 1969	Face the Nation (CBS)	Sen. Mike Mansfield	Interview
June 15, 1969	Issues and Answers (ABC)	Sen. Everett Dirksen, Senate Minority Leader	Interview
June 22, 1969	Face the Nation (CBS)	Rep. Gerald Ford, House Minority Leader	Interview
Sept. 7, 1969	Issues and Answers (ABC)	Rep. Gerald Ford	Interview
Sept. 9, 1969	Today (NBC)	Sen. Everett Dirksen	Informal interview
Sept. 9, 1969	Today (NBC)	Rep. Gerald Ford	Informal interview
Sept. 14, 1969	Issues and Answers (ABC)	Sen. Mike Mansfield	Interview
Sept. 14, 1969	Meet the Press (NBC)	Sen. Hugh Scott, Senate Minority Leader	Interview
Sept. 25, 1969	Today (NBC)	Sen. Hugh Scott	Informal interview
Sept. 28, 1969	Face the Nation (CBS)	Sen. Hugh Scott	Interview
Nov. 9, 1969	Issues and Answers (ABC)	Sen. Hugh Scott	Interview
Jan. 6, 1970	Today (NBC)	Sen. Mike Mansfield	Informal interview
Feb. 1, 1970	Issues and Answers (ABC)	Sen. Mike Mansfield	Interview
Feb. 8, 1970	State of the Union: A Democratic View (ABC, CBS, 1:00–2:00 P.M.; NBC 2:30–3:30 P.M.)	12 Democratic senators, 8 Democratic congressmen	Special (produced by the Democratic Party; film)
Mar. 8, 1970	Face the Nation (CBS)	Sen. Mike Mansfield	Interview
Mar. 20, 1970	Today (NBC)	Sen. Hugh Scott	Informal interview
Mar. 22, 1970	Issues and Answers (ABC)	Sen. Hugh Scott	Interview
Apr. 16, 1970	Today (NBC)	Rep. Gerald Ford	Informal interview

Date	Program	Person	Type
May 17, 1970	Face the Nation (CBS)	Sen. Mike Mansfield	Interview
June 12, 1970	Today (NBC)	Sen. Hugh Scott	Informal interview
June 24, 1970	Response to Nixon address on the economy (NBC, 12:00 M.)	Sen. Mike Mansfield	Address
June 25, 1970	Response to Nixon address on the economy (ABC, 12:00 M.)	Sen. Mike Mansfield	Address
June 28, 1970	Issues and Answers (ABC)	Rep. Gerald Ford	Interview
Nov. 22, 1970	Issues and Answers (ABC, one-hour special)	Sen. Hugh Scott, Sen. Mike Mansfield	Interview
Nov. 26, 1970	Today (NBC)	Sen. Hugh Scott	Informal interview
Jan. 3, 1971	Issues and Answers (ABC)	Rep. John McCormack	Interview
Jan. 4, 1971	Today (NBC)	Rep. John McCormack	Informal interview
Jan. 24, 1971	Meet the Press (NBC)	Rep. Carl Albert, Speaker of the House	Interview
Jan. 24, 1971	Face the Nation (CBS)	Sen. Mike Mansfield	Interview
Jan. 26, 1971	The State of the Union: A Democratic Reply (ABC, CBS, NBC, PBS, 10:00–11:00 P.M.)	Sen. Mike Mansfield	Interview with 4 network correspondents
Mar. 26, 1971	Today (NBC)	Rep. Gerald Ford	Informal interview
Mar. 28, 1971	Meet the Press (NBC)	Sen. Mike Mansfield	Interview
July 3, 1971	American Revolution Bicentennial Era (ABC, CBS, NBC)	Rep. Carl Albert	News special
July 18, 1971	Issues and Answers (ABC)	Sen. Hugh Scott	Interview

This list includes network appearances made by the Senate Majority and Minority Leaders, the Speaker of the House, and the House Minority Leader. Programs include the weekly interview shows ("Meet the Press," "Face the Nation," and "Issues and Answers"), the "Today" show, and special network news broadcasts. Sources: ABC, CBS, NBC, and the offices of the congressional leaders.

Proposed Right of Response Legislation

THE FOLLOWING PROPOSED LEGISLATION establishes a right of response to presidential appearances for the opposition political party during the ninety days prior to a congressional election and during a period commencing January 1 before a presidential election (if the opposition's own presidential candidate, if any, would not already be entitled as a result of the president's appearance to broadcast time under present "equal time" provisions). During these periods, the major opposition party is given a right to "equal opportunities" when the president uses a radio or television station. "Equal opportunities" is defined to provide reasonably equal broadcast time in terms of length and audience potential of the time period. If the president has chosen the format of his appearance, the opposition party may choose its format; if the president's appearance has been carried simultaneously, the opposition party response is to be carried simultaneously also. Exceptions to the opposition party response right are provided for presidential appearances in newscasts or news documentaries and on-the-spot coverage of news events where the president's appearance is incidental.

The proposed legislation also establishes an exemption from the "equal time" requirement (i.e., when one candidate is allowed to use a broadcast station, the station licensee must allow all other legally qualified candidates for the office "equal opportunities") for appearances of a candidate in an opposition party response to a presidential broadcast.

Additions to existing law are underlined; not all portions of the existing statutory language is set out.

A BILL

To amend Section 315 of the
Communications Act of 1934

Be it enacted in the Senate and House of Representatives of the United States of America in Congress assembled.

Sec. 101(a). Section 315(a) of the Commissions Act of 1934 is amended to read as follows:

"(a) If any licensee shall permit any person who is a legally qualified candidate for any public office to use a broadcasting station, he shall afford equal opportunities to all other such candidates for that office in the use of such broadcasting station. . . . Appearance by a legally qualified candidate on any—

(1) bona fide newscast,

(2) bona fide news interview,

(3) bona fide news documentary (if the appearance of the candidate is incidental to the presentation of the subject or subjects covered by the news documentary),

(4) on-the-spot coverage of bona fide news events (including but not limited to political conventions and activities incidental thereto), or

(5) <u>broadcast time made available pursuant to subsection (b) of this section,</u>

shall not be deemed to be use of a broadcasting station within the meaning of this subsection. Nothing in the foregoing sentence shall be construed as relieving broadcasters, in connection with the presentation of newscasts, news interviews, news documentaries, and on-the-spot coverage of news events, from the obligation imposed upon them under this Act to operate in the public interest and to afford reasonable opportunity for the discussion of conflicting views on issues of public importance."

(b). Section 315(b) of such Act is amended to read as

follows:

"(b) If the facilities of any broadcasting station are used by the president of the United States within a period of ninety days preceding a general election of members of the House and Senate of the United States or, in a year in which a presidential election is to be held, within a period commencing January 1 of such year and ending on the day of such election, and if subsection (a) of this section is not applicable to such use, then the licensee of such station shall afford equal opportunities to the national committee of the major opposition political party. Appearances by the president on any—

(1) bona fide newcast,

(2) bona fide news documentary (if the appearance is incidental to the presentation of the subject or subjects covered by the news documentary), or

(3) on-the-spot coverage of bona fide news events (if the appearance is incidental to the event), shall not be deemed to be use of a broadcasting station within the meaning of this subsection.

(c) Present Section 315(f) of such Act is amended to read as follows:

.   .   .   .

(3) For the purposes of subsection (b) of this section, 'major opposition political party' shall mean the political party whose nominees for president and vice-president of the United States received the second-most popular votes in the last presidential election; 'equal opportunities' shall mean a time period the length and scheduling of which is reasonably equal in audience potential to that used by the president and a choice of program format if the president's use consisted of a format chosen by him; provided that where the president's use of a broadcasting station occurs simultaneously with his use of other broadcasting stations, 'equal opportunities' shall also include the same simultaneous carriage."

(d) Present Sections 315(b) through (f) of such Act are redesignated as Sections 315(c) through (g) respectively.

Proposed Voters' Time Legislation

THE FOLLOWING PROPOSED LEGISLATION [1] establishes "Voters' Time"—simultaneous radio, television, and CATV transmission of appearances by major and minor party candidates for president and vice president of the United States in the preelection period. Three party categories are established: category I (the two major parties), category II (strongest minor parties), category III (other significant minor parties). Nominees of category I parties would receive six one-half hour periods of broadcast time, nominees of category II parties would receive two one-half hour periods and category III party nominees would receive one such period. Voters' Time would have to be used by the candidates in a format intended to promote rational discussion and featuring substantial live appearances by the candidate.

The comptroller general of the United States would specify the time periods to be made available for Voters' Time after consultation with broadcasters and CATV system operators. The time used would be paid for by the federal government at not more than 50 percent of the prevailing unit rate for the same type of time or the lowest rate given commercial advertisers, whichever is less.

A BILL

To PROVIDE CERTAIN AMOUNTS OF BROADCAST TIME FOR CANDIDATES FOR PRESIDENT AND VICE PRESIDENT OF THE UNITED STATES.

Be it enacted by the Senate and House of Representatives of the United States of America in Congress assembled,
That part I of title III of the Communications Act of 1934 is amended by adding at the end thereof the following new section:

"VOTERS' TIME

"Definitions

"SEC. 331. (a) For purposes of this section:

"(1) The term 'voters' time' means a period of time required to be made available on a broadcast station or CATV system in accordance with subsection (b) of this section.

"(2) The term 'presidential candidacy' means the candidate of a political party for the office of president of the United States in an election for such office and the candidate of the same party for the office of vice president of the United States in the same election.

"(3) A presidential candidacy is a qualifying presidential candidacy if the individuals who comprise the candidacy (of electors pledged to such individuals) have qualified, more than forty-five days prior to the presidential election, to have their names placed on the official ballot in each of thirty-nine states, except that a presidential candidacy shall not be considered a qualifying presidential candidacy if the combined electoral votes of the states in which the individuals comprising the candidacy (or their electors) have been placed on the ballot are not sufficient to elect a president.

"(4) The term 'CATV system' means a community antenna television system subject to the rules and regulations of the commission, but does not include the automated origination channels of such a system.

"(5) The term 'state' includes the District of Columbia.

"Requirement To Provide Voters' Time

"(b) The facilities of each broadcast station and each CATV system shall be made available at the time periods and rates specified in this section for the purpose of political broadcasts by qualifying presidential candidacies.

"Eligibility for Voters' Time

"(c) Voters' time shall be provided during presidential election campaigns to qualifying presidential candidacies of category I, category II, or category III political parties. For purposes of this section:

"(1) A category I political party is any political party whose presidential candidacy finished first or second in popular votes in at least two of the three most recent presidential elections.

"(2) A category II political party is a political party (other than a category I party) whose presidential candidacy received at least one-eighth of the popular votes cast in the most recent presidential election.

"(3) A category III political party is any political party other than a category I or category II party.

"Specification and Use of Voters' Time

"(d)(1)(A) Prior to each presidential election, the comptroller general of the United States, after consultation with broadcast station licensees and CATV system operators, shall publish in the Federal Register the date and hour of the periods of voters' time which shall be provided to qualifying presidential candidacies by broadcast station licensees and CATV systems. Each period of voters' time provided to a presidential candidacy (i) shall be a half-hour period; (ii) shall be provided to such candidacy at the same date and hour (determined by local time) by all licensees and CATV systems in all of the States, so that voters' time is provided simultaneously within each community by every licensee and CATV system within such community; and (iii) shall be within the thirty-five-day period ending on the day preceding the presidential election and within the hours of 7 o'clock postmeridian to 11 o'clock postmeridian, local time.

"(B) Periods of voters' time shall be allocated to qualifying presidential candidacies as follows:

"(i) The qualifying presidential candidacy of each category I political party shall receive six one-half-hour periods of voters' time during the thirty-five-day period specified in subparagraph (A).

"(ii) The qualifying presidential candidacy of each category II political party shall receive two one-half-hour periods of voters' time during such thirty-five-day period.

"(iii) The qualifying presidential candidacy of each category III political party shall receive one one-half-hour period of voters' time during such thirty-five-day period.
The same presidential candidacy shall not be allocated more than one one-half-hour period of voters' time within any five-day period.

"(2) Voters' time shall be used only for presentations which consist primarily of a substantial live appearance by one or both of the individuals comprising a presidential candidacy in a format intended to promote rational political discussion, clarify major campaign issues, or provide insights into the abilities and personal qualities of the candidates. If the comptroller general finds, upon investigation of a complaint by any person, that a voters' time appearance by a presidential candidacy has not met the criteria of this paragraph, he shall withdraw the allocation of the next one-half-hour period allocated to that candidacy. If the candidacy was allocated only one one-half-hour period, or if the complaint was directed at the last remaining one-half-hour period allocated to the candidacy before the election, the comptroller general shall reduce by one any period of voters' time allocated to a candidacy of the same political party in a subsequent election.

"(3) Broadcast station licensees and CATV systems shall have no power of censorship over the material broadcast or transmitted under the provisions of this section.

"Financing of Voters' Time

"(e)(1) Licensees of broadcast stations (other than noncommercial educational broadcast stations, as defined in section 397(7) of this act) and CATV systems may charge the United States for voters' time used by any qualifying presidential candidacy entitled thereto under this section. Such charge may not exceed the lesser of (A) the lowest unit charge of the broadcast station or CATV system for the same class and amount of time for the same period; or (B) 50 per centum of the lowest published rate of the station or system which would be applicable to a commercial advertiser for such time. Licensees of noncommercial educational broadcast stations may charge the United States with the direct costs incurred in providing voters' time. No additional charges shall be made by broadcast station licensees or CATV systems for the provision of voters' time.

"(2) To secure payment for voters' time, a broadcast station licensee or CATV system shall file with the comptroller general of the United States a statement specifying the dates and amounts of voters' time provided, the rate charged for each period of voters' time, and the total amount due the licensee or CATV system. Upon receipt of the statement, the comptroller general shall verify it by means of such procedures he may establish and, if the statement is found to be valid and legal, shall certify it to the secretary of the Treasury for payment.

"(3) The secretary of the Treasury is hereby authorized and directed to pay in full amount all duly certified statements for voters' time not more than fifteen days following their receipt from the Comptroller General.

"Exemption from Section 315 and from Campaign Spending Limitations

"(f)(1) The provisions of section 315 of this act shall not apply to the use of broadcast station facilities for voters' time under this section.

"(2) The provisions of section 104 of the Federal Election Campaign Act of 1971 shall not apply to expenditures made for the use of voters' time under this section.

"Regulations

"(g) The commission shall prescribe such regulations as may be necessary or appropriate to insure that broadcast licensees, CATV systems, and communications common carriers (whether or not engaged in interstate or foreign communication) cooperate in the arrangements necessary to achieve the simultaneous provision of voters' time within each community as specified by subsection (d)(1) of this section."

NOTES

CHAPTER 1
Politics and Television

1. John J. O'Connor, *New York Times,* August 18, 1971, p. 75.
2. 1970 Annual Report of the Corporation for Public Broadcasting, p. 1.
3. Ben H. Bagdikian, *The Information Machines* (New York: Harper & Row, Publishers, 1971), p. 183.
4. *Broadcasting,* February 14, 1972, p. 38.
5. Nicholas Johnson, *How to Talk Back to Your Television Set* (New York: Bantam Books, 1970), p. 11.
6. Bagdikian, *Information Machines,* p. 183.
7. Special Subcommittee on Investigations, House Committee on Interstate and Foreign Commerce, Report, 91st Cong., 1st sess. (1969), p. 6.
8. *Broadcasting,* April 5, 1971, p. 24, and April 10, 1972, p. 88.
9. Bagdikian, *Information Machines,* p. 13.
10. Erik Barnouw, *The Image Empire* (New York: Oxford University Press, 1970), p. 3.
11. Jay Weitzner, "Handling the Candidate on Television," in *The Political Image Merchants: Strategies in the New Politics,* ed. Ray Hiebert et al. (Washington, D.C.: Acropolis Books, 1971), p. 102.
12. Elihu Katz, "Platforms and Windows: Broadcasting's Role in Election Campaigns," *Journalism Quarterly* (Summer 1971), pp. 304, 308.
13. Early in the fall campaign of 1972, Sen. George McGovern, the Democratic nominee for president, confined his campaign almost entirely to three "media events" a day. That is, he did almost nothing but travel to three television population centers, often widely scattered, to read a statement or make an appearance calculated to provide good

television pictures for the evening news. Once, for example, he traveled to Superior, Wisconsin, and Duluth, Minnesota, to make a statement about the sale of wheat to the Soviet Union that he could have made far more easily from his Washington headquarters. He went to Duluth-Superior solely to be photographed issuing the statement in front of a grain elevator (and, of course, because Wisconsin and Minnesota were states he hoped to win). Before long, however, newspaper reporters began to complain that McGovern was running a phony campaign of little substance, television reporters began to view his calculated performances skeptically, and his advisers concluded he must change his style. He did, addressing large political rallies and delivering serious half-hour speeches on major issues to the evening television audience. McGovern's experience led some observers to wonder whether the power of television in political campaigns was waning. Others concluded that McGovern simply used it too blatantly.

14. See studies cited in The Twentieth Century Fund Commission on Campaign Costs in the Electronic Era, *Voters' Time* (New York: Twentieth Century Fund, 1969), pp. 55–58, nn. 1–2.

15. *Washington Post,* June 18, 1971, p. A2.

16. *Washington Post,* November 22, 1970, p. A1.

17. *Time,* May 18, 1971, p. 18.

18. *New York Times,* May 10, 1971, p. 33.

19. Committee for Economic Development, *Financing a Better Election System* (December 1968), p. 41.

20. Revenue Act of 1971 (Public Law 92–178, 85 Stat. 497).

21. Federal Election Campaign Act of 1971 (Public Law 92–225, 86 Stat. 3).

22. Hearings on S.J. Res. 209 before the Communications Subcommittee of the Senate Committee on Commerce, 91st Cong., 2d sess., ser. no. 91–74 (1970), p. 40.

23. Quoted in William L. Rivers, "Appraising Press Coverage of Politics," in *Politics and the Press,* ed. Richard W. Lee (Washington, D.C.: Acropolis Books, 1970), p. 53.

24. Richard E. Neustadt, *Presidential Power* (New York: John Wiley & Sons, Inc., 1960), p. 10.

25. 116 *Congressional Record,* S81612 (daily ed., June 2, 1970).

26. *Youngstown Sheet & Tube Co.* v. *Sawyer,* 343 U.S. 579, 653–54 (1952) (concurring opinion by Justice Jackson).

27. Clinton Rossiter, *The American Presidency* (New York: New American Library, 1962), p. 66.

28. Wilson P. Dizard, *Television: A World View* (Syracuse, N.Y.: Syracuse University Press, 1967), p. 149.

29. Address by Richard S. Salant, president of CBS News, before the Journalism Foundation of Metropolitan St. Louis, May 1, 1972.

30. Committee for Fair Broadcasting of Controversial Issues, quoted in Comment, "Televised Presidential Addresses and the FCC's Fairness Doctrine," *Columbia Journal of Law and Social Problems* 7 (1971): 75, 79.

31. *Broadcasting,* September 20, 1971, p. 32.

32. Ibid.

33. Remarks of Richard W. Jencks, president of CBS/Broadcast Group, before the Federal Communications Bar Association, Washington, D.C., June 16, 1971.

34. Address by Hon. Dean Burch, Chairman, Federal Communications Commission, to the National Association of Broadcasters, Chicago, Illinois, March 31, 1971.

35. House of Representatives Report No. 464, p. 3, 69th Cong., 1st sess. (1926).

36. Remarks of Sen. John O. Pastore, Hearings on S.J. Res. 209, p. 2.

CHAPTER 2
The Bully Pulpit

1. Hearings on S.J. Res. 209 before the Communications Subcommittee of the Senate Committee on Commerce, 91st Cong., 2d sess., ser. no. 91–74 (1970), p. 19.

2. From a Louis Harris study introduced in Hearings on S.J. Res. 209, p. 20.

3. *New York Times,* June 25, 1970, p. 44.

4. Letter from Democratic National Committee to William B. Ray, Federal Communications Commission, July 23, 1970.

5. Complaint by the Black Congressmen of the House of Representatives to the FCC, February 1, 1972, p. 14.

6. *Time,* November 3, 1924, p. 1.

7. *Time,* January 18, 1971, p. 36.

8. Les Brown, *Television: The Business behind the Box* (New York: Harcourt Brace Jovanovich, 1971), p. 58.

9. *Democratic National Committee,* 25 FCC 2d 216, 231 (1970).

10. Robert MacNeil, *The People Machine* (New York: Harper & Row, Publishers, 1968), p. 289.

11. *Broadcasting,* November 24, 1969, p. 54.

12. *Broadcasting,* December 15, 1969, p. 28.

13. "Televised Presidential Addresses and the FCC's Fairness Doctrine," *Columbia Journal of Law and Social Problems* 7 (1971): 75, 83.

14. Edward W. Chester, *Radio, Television and American Politics* (New York: Sheed & Ward, 1969), p. 33.

15. William L. Rivers, "Appraising Press Coverage of Politics," in *Politics and the Press,* ed. Richard W. Lee (Washington, D.C.: Acropolis Books, 1970), p. 52.

16. Pierre Salinger, *With Kennedy* (New York: Avon Books, 1967), p. 185.

17. Samuel L. Becker, "Presidential Power: The Influence of Broadcasting," *Quarterly Journal of Speech* 47 (February 1961): 10, 11.

18. William L. Rivers, *The Opinionmakers* (Boston: Beacon Press, 1967), p. 100.

19. Chester, *Radio, Television and American Politics,* p. 16.

20. Becker, "Presidential Power," pp. 10, 12.
21. Chester, *Radio, Television and American Politics*, p. 23.
22. Becker, "Presidential Power," pp. 10, 12; Chester, *Radio, Television and American Politics*, p. 23.
23. The story is attributed by Leo Rosten to Alistair Cooke. *World,* August 15, 1972, p. 13.
24. Chester, *Radio, Television and American Politics*, p. 28.
25. Ibid.
26. Elmer E. Cornwell, Jr., *Presidential Leadership of Public Opinion* (Bloomington: Indiana University Press, 1965), p. 255.
27. Address by Richard S. Salant, president of CBS News, to the Journalism Foundation of Metropolitan St. Louis, May 1, 1972.
28. Erik Barnouw, *The Golden Web* (New York: Oxford University Press, 1968), p. 170.
29. *Broadcasting,* February 14, 1972, p. 68.
30. Quoted in Arthur M. Schlesinger, Jr., *The Age of Roosevelt* (Boston: Houghton, Mifflin Co., 1957), Vol. 2.
31. Chester, *Radio, Television and American Politics*, p. 33.
32. Quoted in Cornwell, *Presidential Leadership*, p. 259.
33. Quoted in Rivers, *Opinionmakers*, p. 137.
34. Chester, *Radio, Television and American Politics*, p. 32.
35. Barnouw, *Golden Web*, p. 152.
36. Ibid., p. 7.
37. Ibid., p. 211.
38. Chester, *Radio, Television and American Politics*, pp. 32–33.
39. In his "Fireside Chats" on April 28, 1935; March 9, 1937; April 14, 1938; and April 28, 1942, among others, Roosevelt sought support for various legislative proposals.
40. Barnouw, *Golden Web*, p. 7.
41. Leila A. Sussman, "FDR and the White House Mail," *Public Opinion Quarterly* 20 (Spring 1956): 16.
42. Wilfred E. Binkley, *President and Congress* (New York: Vantage Books, 1962), p. 305.
43. Sussman, "FDR and the White House Mail," p. 14.
44. James MacGregor Burns, *Roosevelt: The Lion and the Fox* (New York: Harcourt, Brace & Co., 1956), p. 227.
45. Chester, *Radio, Television and American Politics*, pp. 34–41.
46. Ibid.
47. Becker, "Presidential Power," pp. 10, 15.
48. *Broadcasting,* October 18, 1971, p. 52.
49. Robert S. Allen and William V. Shannon, *Truman Merry-Go-Round* (New York: Vanguard Press, 1950), p. 35.
50. Chester, *Radio, Television and American Politics*, p. 75.
51. Richard E. Neustadt, *Presidential Power* (New York: John Wiley & Sons, Inc., 1960), p. 19.
52. Stanley Kelley, *Professional Public Relations and Political Power* (Baltimore: The Johns Hopkins Press, 1956), pp. 160–61.
53. Cornwell, *Presidential Leadership*, p. 270.
54. Interview, Washington, D.C., June 23, 1971.

NOTES 205

55. Martin Mayer, "How Television News Covers the World (In 4,000 Words or Less)," *Esquire,* January 1972.
56. MacNeil, *People Machine,* pp. 305–6; *New York Times,* February 28, 1958, p. 45.
57. *Broadcasting,* November 8, 1965, p. 55, lists all live appearances by President Eisenhower covered by one or more networks, exclusive of presidential campaign appearances.
58. Chester, *Radio, Television and American Politics,* p. 92.
59. *Wall Street Journal,* August 19, 1953, quoted in Kelley, *Professional Public Relations,* p. 2.
60. Neustadt, *Presidential Power,* pp. 71–72.
61. Chester, *Radio, Television and American Politics,* p. 105.
62. Erik Barnouw, *The Image Empire* (New York: Oxford University Press, 1970), pp. 94–99.
63. Rivers, *Opinionmakers,* pp. 141–42.
64. Barnouw, *Image Empire,* p. 78.
65. Theodore C. Sorensen, *Kennedy* (New York: Harper & Row, 1965), p. 331.
66. "A more important factor . . . was the editorial opposition we were certain to encounter from a majority of the newspapers on domestic policy. . . . The publishers of seven out of ten dailies had come out for Nixon. We could expect them to hold their fire for a time, at least, on foreign policy. But we could also expect immediate and powerful opposition . . . to his early plans for stimulating the economy and resolving the volatile civil rights issue. FDR, when he was under strongest attack, took his case directly to the people. . . . I felt JFK would have to do the same eventually—and live TV was the way to do it" (Salinger, *With Kennedy,* p. 83).
67. Ibid., p. 79.
68. Harry Sharp, Jr., "Live from Washington: The Telecasting of President Kennedy's News Conference," *Journal of Broadcasting* 13 (Winter 1968): 25.
69. Salinger, *With Kennedy,* p. 85.
70. Ibid., p. 83.
71. Sharp, "Live from Washington," pp. 25, 27–28.
72. Sorensen, *Kennedy,* pp. 322, 325.
73. William Small, *To Kill a Messenger: Television News and the Real World* (New York: Hastings House, 1970), p. 27.
74. Cornwell, *Presidential Leadership,* p. 283.
75. Sorensen, *Kennedy,* p. 324.
76. Pierre Salinger, quoted in Bernard Rubin, *Political Television* (Belmont, Calif.: Wadsworth Publishing Co., 1967), p. 82.
77. Quoted in Rubin, *Political Television,* p. 84.
78. Jules Witcover, "Salvaging the Presidential Press Conference," *Columbia Journalism Review* (Fall 1970): 31.
79. Arthur M. Schlesinger, Jr., *A Thousand Days* (Boston: Houghton Mifflin Co., 1965), p. 717.
80. Quoted in Rubin, *Political Television,* p. 84.
81. *Broadcasting,* November 8, 1965, p. 55, lists all appearances by

President Kennedy carried live by one or more of the television networks.

82. Salinger, *With Kennedy,* p. 155.

83. Ibid., pp. 332–33.

84. Rubin, *Political Television,* pp. 92–93.

85. Interview, William Small, CBS News, Washington, D.C., June 21, 1971.

86. *Time,* March 1, 1964, p. 19.

87. Interview, New York City, July 22, 1971.

88. Small, *To Kill a Messenger,* pp. 232–33.

89. The studio was first used on February 4, 1965, when Johnson held a televised news conference before two hundred newsmen. In order to allow the president to make spur-of-the-moment appearances, the networks kept the studio manned five and a half days a week (during the hours the White House Press Office was open) at an estimated cost of more than $50,000 annually. After his first few telecasts, the president used the studio only rarely and—with the approval of the White House —the networks ended full staffing late in 1966. During the Nixon administration, it was abandoned altogether.

90. Small, *To Kill a Messenger,* pp. 240 ff.

91. Gene Wyckoff, *The Image Candidates* (New York: The Macmillan Co., 1968), p. 243.

92. Barnouw, *Image Empire,* p. 285.

93. *Broadcasting,* November 8, 1965, p. 58.

94. *Public Papers of the Presidents of the United States, Richard Nixon, 1969* (Washington, D.C.: Government Printing Office, 1971), p. 246.

95. For a detailed account of the Hiss-Chambers case told from Nixon's point of view, see Richard Nixon, *Six Crises* (New York: Pyramid Books, 1968), pp. 1–76.

96. Earl Mazo, *Richard Nixon: A Political and Personal Portrait* (New York: Harper Bros., 1959), p. 122.

97. Ibid., p. 135.

98. Quoted in Kurt and Gladys Lang, *Politics and Television* (Chicago: Quadrangle Books, 1968), p. 29.

99. Mazo, *Richard Nixon,* p. 134.

100. Kelley, *Professional Public Relations,* p. 224.

101. Barnouw, *Image Empire,* p. 79.

102. Charles A. H. Thomson and Frances M. Shattuck, *The 1956 Presidential Campaign* (Washington, D.C.: The Brookings Institution, 1960), p. 342.

103. Quoted in Mazo, *Richard Nixon,* p. 299. During his 1960 presidential campaign, Nixon began one of his paid campaign broadcasts with an apology to viewers for replacing the regularly scheduled program.

104. Nixon, *Six Crises,* p. 384.

105. Ibid.

106. Barnouw, *Image Empire,* p. 169.

107. Theodore White, *The Making of the President 1960* (New York: Atheneum, 1961), p. 289.

108. Nixon, *Six Crises*, p. 366.
109. Ibid., p. 457.
110. *Time,* October 12, 1962, p. 25.
111. Quoted in Ralph de Toledano, *One Man Alone: Richard Nixon* (New York: Funk & Wagnalls, 1969), p. 319.
112. Theodore White, *The Making of the President 1968* (New York: Atheneum, 1969), p. 131.
113. Remarks delivered to the International Association of Political Consultants, Royal Garden Hotel, London, England, December 14, 1970.
114. Hearings on S.J. Res. 209, p. 64.
115. Address by Richard S. Salant, president of CBS News, to the Journalism Foundation of Metropolitan St. Louis, May 1, 1972.
116. Unless otherwise indicated, all audience figures are from A. C. Nielsen Company data supplied by the White House Press Office, NBC, or the A. C. Nielsen Company.
117. During his first eighteen months in office, President Kennedy made fifty network television appearances. Most were daytime news conferences; only four were in prime time. During a comparable time period, President Nixon made only thirty-seven appearances on television, but fourteen were prime time news conferences and addresses (see Appendix A, Table 1).
118. Address by Frank Stanton, president of CBS, to the 1970 National Broadcast Editorial Conference, Park City, Utah, July 10, 1970.
119. *Time,* January 18, 1971, p. 36.
120. Ibid.
121. *Broadcasting,* December 28, 1970, p. 9.
122. "Weekly Compilation of Presidential Documents" 7:943 (1971).
123. *Public Papers of the President 1969,* p. 301.
124. Had he delivered a major television address during the campaign without mentioning the Vietnam issue, he would have been severely criticized, for it was the country's overriding concern. He has been represented as unwilling to discuss it, since to do so would have destroyed the confidentiality of the talks between his negotiator and Hanoi's.
125. President Nixon once told a press conference from which television was barred that "television has probably had as much of the President as it wants at this point, and that is why you are getting this kind of conference" (*New York Times,* February 11, 1972).
126. "Weekly Compilation of Presidential Documents" 6:724 (1970).
127. *Public Papers of the President 1969,* p. 909.
128. "Weekly Compilation of Presidential Documents" 6:721–25 (1970).
129. Interview, Washington, D.C., September 23, 1970.
130. Quoted by FCC Commissioner Nicholas Johnson in remarks before the International Association of Political Consultants, Royal Garden Hotel, London, England, December 14, 1970.
131. Complaint of fourteen U.S. Senators and Amendment to End the War Committee, filed with the FCC July 8, 1970.

132. "Weekly Compilation of Presidential Documents" 6:78 (1970).
133. *Broadcasting,* February 2, 1970, p. 56.
134. "Weekly Compilation of Presidential Documents" 6:774–81 (1970).
135. *Public Papers of the President 1969,* p. 369.
136. Ibid., p. 906.
137. Ibid., p. 809.
138. Don Oberdorfer, "A Dying Institution?" *Washington Post,* November 19, 1970, p. A19.
139. *Broadcasting Yearbook, 1971* (Washington, D.C.: Broadcasting Publications, Inc., 1971), p. A121.
140. Letter from Democratic National Committee to William B. Ray, FCC, April 13, 1971.
141. Brief of Petitioner, Democratic National Committee, at 5, *Democratic National Committee v. FCC,* 460 F.2d 1018 (D.C. Cir. 1972).
142. Quoted in *Politics and the Press,* ed. Lee, pp. 95–96.
143. *Washington Post,* June 1, 1971, p. A1; *Broadcasting Yearbook, 1971* (Washington, D.C.: Broadcasting Publications, Inc., 1971), p. A121. This figure prompted President Nixon to order cuts in executive branch public relations expenditures, calling some public relations efforts "a questionable use of the taxpayers' money for the purpose of promoting and soliciting support for various agency activities."
144. *Washington Post,* February 20, 1972, p. B7.
145. *Broadcasting,* February 14, 1972, p. 45.
146. *New York Times,* February 25, 1972, p. 4.
147. *Chicago Sun Times,* March 5, 1972, sec. 2, p. 7.
148. *Washington Star,* February 29, 1972, p. A1.
149. *Chicago Daily News,* March 4, 1972.
150. *Broadcasting,* March 6, 1972, p. 48.

CHAPTER 3
The Limits of the Law

1. Address by Frank Stanton, president of CBS, to the 1970 National Broadcast Editorial Conference, Park City, Utah, July 10, 1970.
2. *New York Times,* July 8, 1970, p. 1.
3. *U.S. News and World Report,* July 27, 1970, p. 56.
4. Sydney W. Head, *Broadcasting in America* (Boston: Houghton Mifflin Co., 1956), p. 129.
5. Radio Act of 1927, Ch. 169, 44 Stat. 1162.
6. *National Broadcasting Co. v. United States,* 319 U.S. 190, 213 (1942).
7. *Red Lion Broadcasting Co. v. FCC,* 395 U.S. 367, 390 (1969).
8. Federal Communications Commission, *Public Service Responsibility of Broadcast Licensees* (Washington, D.C., March 1956).
9. *Obligation of Licensees to Carry Political Broadcasts,* 25 P & F *Radio Reg.* 1931 (1963).
10. *In the Matter of Loyola University,* 12 P & F *Radio Reg.* 1017,

1099 (1956); *In Re Application of City of Jacksonville,* 12 P & F *Radio Reg.* 113, 180j (1956); *Homer P. Rainey,* 3 P & F *Radio Reg.* 737 (1946).

11. 47 U.S.C. §312(a)(7).

12. Memorandum from FCC General Counsel Henry Geller to the commissioners of the FCC, dated September 2, 1969, reviews the legal ramifications of the case of *Red Lion Broadcasting Company* v. *FCC* 395 U.S. 367 (1969), decided by the Supreme Court three months earlier. The memorandum interprets *Red Lion* as a landmark decision finally settling the controversy over the FCC's legal authority to "interest itself in general program format and the kinds of programs broadcast by licensees."

13. *Notice of Inquiry,* Docket No. 19154, FCC 71–159 (1971).

14. Marvin Barrett, ed., *Survey of Broadcast Journalism 1970–1971* (New York: Grosset & Dunlap, 1971), p. 13.

15. H. R. Rep. 464, 69th Cong., 1st sess. (1926), p. 16.

16. Communications Act of 1934, 47 U.S.C. §315:

(a) If any licensee shall permit any person who is a legally qualified candidate for any public office to use a broadcasting station, he shall afford equal opportunities to all such candidates for that office in the use of such broadcasting station: PROVIDED, That such licensee shall have no power of censorship over the material broadcast under the provisions of this section. No obligation is imposed under this subsection upon any licensee to allow the use of its station by any such candidate. Appearance by a legally qualified candidate on any

(1) bona fide newscast

(2) bona fide news interview

(3) bona fide news documentary (if the appearance of the candidate is incidental to the presentation of the subject or subjects covered by the news documentary), or

(4) on-the-spot coverage of bona fide news events (including but not limited to political conventions and activities incidental thereto),

shall not be deemed to be use of a broadcasting station within the meaning of this subsection. Nothing in the foregoing sentence shall be construed as relieving broadcasters, in connection with the presentation of newscasts, news interviews, news documentaries, and on-the-spot coverage of news events, from the obligation imposed upon them under this chapter to operate in the public interest and to afford reasonable opportunity for the discussion of conflicting views on issues of public importance. . . .

(g) The Commission shall prescribe appropriate rules and regulations to carry out the provisions of this section.

17. A licensee cannot limit a candidate to a particular format once his opponent has appeared on the licensee's facilities. "The basic objective of Section 315 [is] to permit a candidate to present himself to the electorate in a manner wholly unfettered by licensee judgment . . ." Gray Communications Systems, Inc., 19 FCC 2d 532 (1969); Pacific Broadcasting Co., 32 FCC 2d 273 (1971).

18. Hearings on Political Broadcasting before the Communications Subcommittee of the Senate Committee on Commerce, 86th Cong., 1st sess. (1959); S. Rep. No. 562, 86th Cong., 1st sess. (1959); H. R. Rep. No. 802, 86th Cong., 1st sess. (1959); Pub. L. 86–274, 73 Stat. 557.

19. *Use of Broadcast Facilities by Candidates for Public Office,* FCC 66–386, 31 F.R. 6660, 6663–7 (May 4, 1966).

20. *Greater New York Broadcasting Corp.,* 40 FCC 235 (1946). "The right to equal opportunity in the use of broadcast facilities runs in favor of a legally qualified candidate representing a party, not in favor of that party itself." *National Laugh Party,* 40 FCC 289 (1957).

21. *Columbia Broadcasting System, Inc.,* 40 FCC 395 (1964).

22. *United Community Campaigns of America,* 40 FCC 390 (1964).

23. *In Re Section 315,* 40 FCC 276 (1956).

24. *Republican National Committee,* 40 FCC 408 (1964); *aff'd per curiam by equally divided Court sub. nom. Goldwater* v. *FCC,* No. 18, 963 (D.C. Cir. 1964), *cert. den.,* 379 U.S. 893 (1964).

25. Recognizing this problem, Congress in 1960 temporarily suspended section 315 to make possible the "Great Debates" between candidates Nixon and Kennedy (Public Law 86–677, 74 Stat. 554).

26. *Thirty-third Annual Report,* Federal Communications Commission, quoted in House Committee on Interstate and Foreign Commerce, Special Subcommittee on Investigations, "The Fairness Doctrine and Related Issues," H.R. Rep. No. 91–257, 91st Cong., 1st sess. (1969), p. 12. The statutory basis for fairness is 47 U.S.C. §315 (a).

27. Robert V. Cahill, "Fairness and the FCC," 21 Fed. Comm. B.J. 17, 19 (1967).

28. *Cullman Broadcasting Co., Inc.,* 40 FCC 576 (1963).

29. *WCBS-TV,* 8 FCC 2d 381 (1967).

30. *University of Houston,* 11 FCC 2d 790 (1968).

31. *Committee for Fair Broadcasting of Controversial Issues,* 25 FCC 2d 283 (1970).

32. *Station WCBS-TV,* 9 FCC 2d 921 (1967); *Retail Store Employees Union, Local 880* v. *FCC,* 436 F. 2d 248 (D.C. Cir. 1970); *King Broadcasting Co.,* 15 FCC 2d 829 (1967).

33. 47 C.F.R. §§73.123, 73.300, 73.598, 73.679, 76.209.

34. Ibid.

35. *Applicability of the Fairness Doctrine in the Handling of Controversial Issues of Public Importance,* 29 F.R. 10416 (1964).

36. *Committee for the Fair Broadcasting of Controversial Issues,* 25 FCC 2d 283, 294 (1970).

37. *Paul E. Fitzpatrick,* 40 FCC 443 (1950).

38. Ibid.

39. *Washington Bureau NAACP* 40 FCC 479, 480 (1959).

40. *Democratic State Central Committee of California,* 12 P & F Radio Reg. 867 (1960).

41. *California Democratic State Central Committee,* 40 FCC 501 (1960).

42. *Republican National Committee,* 40 FCC 625 (1964); *aff'd per curiam by equally divided Court sub. nom. Goldwater* v. *FCC* No. 18,963 (D.C. Cir. 1964), *cert. den.,* 379 U.S. 893 (1964).

43. *Avco Broadcasting Corp.*, 32 FCC 2d 124 (1971); *National Broadcasting Co.*, 30 FCC 2d (1971).

44. *Committee for the Fair Broadcasting of Controversial Issues*, 25 FCC 2d 283 (1970).

45. "We wish to stress that we are not holding that such an obligation arises from a single speech—that where an uninterrupted address is afforded one side, the fairness doctrine demands that the other side be presented in the same format. . . .

"We wish to emphasize that we are not in any sense addressing ourselves to the matter of equalizing impact. . . . As many of the complainants recognize, the President stands alone in this respect. . . .

"We do not mean to discourage in any way the network's presentation of Presidential reports to the nation. . . . Our holding is limited to the unusual facts of this case—near balance on an issue, with one side in addition afforded five prime time opportunities to deliver speeches on that issue." Ibid., pp. 297–298.

46. Ibid., p. 304.

47. Ibid., p. 298.

48. *Arkansas Radio & Equipment Co.*, 40 FCC 1070 (1960).

49. *Lawrence M.C. Smith*, 40 FCC 549 (1963).

50. *Nicholas Zapple*, 23 FCC 2d 707 (1970).

51. *Republican National Committee*, 25 FCC 2d 739, 744, (1970).

52. *Republican National Committee*, 25 P & F *Radio Reg.* 2d 582 (1972).

CHAPTER 4
Congress, Court, and Camera

1. Seth Goldschlager, "The Supreme Court and the Media: The Reporters and the Reported" (Senior Thesis, Yale University Law School, 1971), pp. 66, 281.

2. Rule 53, *Federal Rules of Criminal Procedure.*

3. *Estes* v. *Texas*, 381 U.S. 532 (1964).

4. 381 U.S. 532, 549.

5. 19 How. 393 (1857).

6. Beitzinger, "Chief Justice Taney and the Publication of Court Opinions," *Catholic University of America Law Review* 7 (1958): 32.

7. *Eisner* v. *Macomber*, 252 U.S. 189 (1920); see Boris I. Bittker, *Federal Income, Estate and Gift Taxation* (Boston: Little, Brown and Co., 1958), p. 63.

8. Goldschlager, "Supreme Court and the Media," pp. 254–56.

9. 370 U.S. 421 (1962).

10. Goldschlager, "Supreme Court and the Media," p. 251.

11. Ibid., pp. 259–66.

12. *U.S. News and World Report*, December 14, 1970, p. 32.

13. Goldschlager, "Supreme Court and the Media," p. 273 ff.

14. Alexander Hamilton, *The Federalist*, No. 78.

15. Alexander M. Bickel, *The Least Dangerous Branch* (Indianapolis: Bobbs-Merrill, 1962), p. 197.

212   NOTES

16. "A Conversation with Earl Warren," WGBH-TV, Boston, Mass., December 11, 1972.
17. 1 Cranch 137, 2 L. ed. 60 (1803).
18. William MacDonald, *Jacksonian Democracy* (New York: Harper & Row, 1968), p. 177.
19. Alexis de Tocqueville, *Democracy in America* (New York: Schocken Books, 1961), Vol. 1, p. 166.
20. Robert H. Jackson, *The Struggle for Judicial Supremacy* (New York: A. A. Knopf, 1941), p. ix.
21. 374 U.S. 483 (1954).
22. Jack W. Peltason, *Fifty-Eight Lonely Men* (New York: Harcourt, Brace & World, 1961), p. 48.
23. *New York Times,* August 4, 1971, p. 1.
24. Alexander Hamilton, *The Federalist,* No. 73.
25. James Madison, *The Federalist,* No. 49.
26. Quoted in Clinton Rossiter, *The American Presidency* (New York: New American Library, 1962), p. 29.
27. Address by Frank Stanton, president of CBS, to the 1970 National Broadcast Editorial Conference, Park City, Utah, July 10, 1970.
28. *Committee for Fair Broadcasting of Controversial Issues,* 25 FCC 2d 283, 310 (1970).
29. Hearings on S.J. Res. 209 before the Communications Subcommittee of the Senate Committee on Commerce, 91st Cong., 2d sess., ser. no. 91–74 (1970), p. 40.
30. Sen. Charles McC. Mathias, Jr. (R–Md.), interviewed on "Thirty Minutes with . . . ," WETA-TV, Washington, D.C., November 30, 1972.
31. Sig Mickelson, *The Electric Mirror* (New York: Dodd, Mead, & Co., 1972), p. 182.
32. John Whale, *The Half-Shut Eye* (London: Macmillan & Co., 1969), p. 101.
33. James Reston, *The Artillery of the Press* (New York: Harper & Row, Publishers, 1967), p. 64.
34. Erik Barnouw, *The Image Empire* (New York: Oxford University Press, 1970), p. 279.
35. Legislative Reorganization Act of 1970, P.L. 91–510, 84 Stat. 1140.
36. *Broadcasting,* June 28, 1971, p. 26.
37. William S. White, *Chicago Tribune,* July 18, 1971.
38. Hearings on S.J. Res. 209, p. 4.
39. Ibid., p. 9.
40. Ibid., p. 73.
41. Ibid., p. 103.
42. Ibid., p. 37.
43. Ibid., p. 96.
44. William L. Rivers, *The Opinionmakers* (Boston: Beacon Press, 1965), p. 100.
45. Erik Barnouw, *The Golden Web* (New York: Oxford University Press, 1968), pp. 48–50.

46. Edward W. Chester, *Radio, Television and American Politics* (New York: Sheed & Ward, 1969), p. 35.

47. Robert MacNeil, *The People Machine* (New York: Harper & Row, Publishers, 1968), p. 248.

48. *Washington Post,* February 23, 1972, p. B15.

49. Figures supplied by Senate Recording Studio, 1971.

50. *Broadcasting,* August 31, 1970, p. 54.

51. Hearings on S.J. Res. 209, p. 36.

52. Ibid. p. 118.

53. Interview, Washington, D.C., July 30, 1971.

54. Interview, Washington, D.C., September 29, 1971.

55. Hearings on S.J. Res. 209, p. 9.

56. Ibid.

57. Address by Frank Stanton, July 10, 1970.

58. ARB New York City ratings listed in "Complaint of Fourteen United States Senators," filed with FCC, July 8, 1970.

59. Letter from CBS to Sen. George McGovern, June 30, 1970.

60. Letter to FCC Chairman Dean Burch, July 8, 1970, p. 7.

61. 116 *Congressional Record,* S11543 (daily ed., July 16, 1970).

62. Complaint and Request for Declaratory Ruling by the Black Congressmen of the House of Representatives of the United States, FCC, February 1, 1972.

63. FCC News Release, Rept. No. 11190, December 21, 1972 (Black Caucus); FCC News Release, Rept. No. 11196, December 22, 1972 (Fourteen Members of Congress).

64. Statement of Sen. Edmund Muskie, Hearings on S.J. Res. 209, p. 41.

65. In April 1973, Senator Mike Mansfield objected to the major networks' refusal to cover a speech by Senator Edmund Muskie intended as a response to a presidential address which had been broadcast by all of the networks. Senator Mansfield argued that the networks "appear to be responsive to threats by members in the executive branch but show no appreciation for an attempt on behalf of Congress to be responsible in shaping the public perceptions and determining significant national decisions." (*The New York Times,* April 4, 1973, p. 26.)

66. Similar live broadcasts from time to time of sessions of the Austrian Parliament have been successful in that country. Televised debate of important national decisions has spurred interest in the subjects debated and has attracted a good audience. Austrian television also presents "From the Parliament," a weekly evening summary of Parliament's activities.

67. It is true that if a senator who is a candidate for reelection delivers a televised address from the floor of the Senate, his opponent back home may be at a disadvantage. Application of the "equal time" law, however, could make televising of the congressional sessions unworkable, for each program could result in a rash of requests for equal time. The ability to speak in congressional debate is an inherent advantage of incumbency; public resentment would soon curb abuses of televised de-

bates for electioneering. The potential value of the programs simply outweighs the possibility of unfairness.
68. *Broadcasting,* September 14, 1970, p. 23.
69. Joseph Story, *Commentaries on the Constitution of the United States* (Boston: Little, Brown and Co., 1958), §§840–41, quoted in Complaint and Request for Declaratory Ruling by the Black Congressmen of the House of Representatives, FCC, February 1, 1972, p. 25.

CHAPTER 5
The Loyal Opposition

1. Lawrence F. O'Brien, "Television Is Threatening Our Democratic Process," *TV Guide,* September 19, 1970, p. 10.
2. Erik Barnouw, *The Golden Web* (New York: Oxford University Press, 1968), p. 14.
3. Ibid., pp. 44–48.
4. Clinton Rossiter, *The American Presidency* (New York: New American Library, 1962), p. 62.
5. Letter from Democratic National Committee to William B. Ray, Federal Communications Commission, April 13, 1971.
6. CBS Letter to William B. Ray, FCC, July 23, 1970.
7. "Rules of the Democratic National Committee," Article I, section 2(d).
8. Petition of the Republican National Committee for Relief, July 13, 1970, *Committee for Fair Broadcasting of Controversial Issues,* 25 FCC 2d 233 (1970).
9. Clarence Cannon, *The Official Democratic Manual* (Washington, D.C.: Democratic National Committee, 1968), p. 10.
10. Interview with George Reedy, Washington, D.C., September 17, 1971.
11. Interview with Frederick Dutton, Washington, D.C., September 30, 1971.
12. Interview with Ronald Ziegler, Washington, D.C., August 11, 1971.
13. Interview with Peter Lisagor, Washington, D.C., August 6, 1971.
14. Ben H. Bagdikian, *The Information Machines* (New York: Harper & Row, Publishers, 1971), p. 59.
15. Other network programs featuring interviews with political figures with some regularity are "Today," "CBS Morning News," "The Merv Griffin Show," "The Dick Cavett Show," and "The Mike Douglas Show." Nearly all such programs are presented outside of prime television viewing hours and have relatively small audiences.
16. This has not always been true, however. In 1965, Republican Rep. Catherine May charged that for the first six months of that year, CBS had presented one "out" Republican and fourteen "in" Democrats on "Face the Nation"; NBC had five Republicans and twelve Democrats on "Meet the Press"; and ABC presented six Republicans and nineteen Democrats on "Issues and Answers" (*Broadcasting,* July 26, 1965, p.

56). Likewise, a 1966 study by the Republican Congressional Committee claimed that during two weeks in June and August of that year respectively, the party network exposure was:

	JUNE WEEK (IN MINUTES)		AUGUST WEEK (IN MINUTES)	
	Democrats	Republicans	Democrats	Republicans
NBC	87.00	23.20	168.24	13.56
CBS	84.15	38.30	192.50	34.50
ABC	100.20	6.45	115.00	6.00

(From Robert MacNeil, *The People Machine*, p. 250.)

17. Interview, Washington, D.C., August 6, 1971.

18. In January 1972, the networks did make time available, on request, to Democratic congressmen to respond to the president's State of the Union address. But the time was made available to the congressional opposition rather than to the party as such.

19. This figure represents only instances in which format and content were under the control of the national committee of the opposition party, such as the CBS "Loyal Opposition" program in July 1970. It does not include time made available to Congress to respond to the president's State of the Union address.

20. This figure represents only the appearances of administration officials on "Meet the Press," "Face the Nation," and "Issues and Answers" during the first twelve months of the Nixon administration.

21. DNC News Release, August 15, 1971, p. 7.

22. DNC Request for Declaratory Ruling, filed with FCC May 19, 1970, pp. 8–9.

23. Ibid., p. 14.

24. *Democratic National Committee*, 25 FCC 2d 216 (1970).

25. Brief of the DNC, Business Executives' Move for Vietnam Peace v. FCC, 450 F. 2d 642 (D.C. Cir. 1971). The case bears this name because the DNC appeal had been consolidated with a BEM appeal of an FCC denial of its complaint against station WTOP in Washington, D.C., which had refused to sell the organization time to broadcast antiwar advertisements. WTOP had cited "its long established policy of refusing to sell spot announcement time to individuals or groups to set forth views on controversial issues." Cf. *Business Executives' Move for Vietnam Peace*, 25 FCC 2d 242 (1970).

26. *Business Executives' Move for Vietnam Peace* v. *FCC*, 450 F. 2d 642 (D.C. Cir. 1971), 41 U.S.L.W. 4688 (U.S. May 29, 1973).

27. "Weekly Compilation of Presidential Documents" 6:1539 (November 1, 1970).

28. *Broadcasting*, November 9, 1970, p. 24.

29. Ibid., pp. 23–25; interview with Geoffrey Cowan, Washington, D.C., November 8, 1971.

30. Brief of DNC, Democratic National Committee v. FCC, 460 F. 2d 891 (D.C. Cir. 1972), *cert. den.*, 93 S.Ct. 42 (1972).

31. Letter from DNC to William B. Ray, FCC, April 13, 1971.
32. *Broadcasting,* March 29, 1971, p. 15.
33. Telegram from DNC to Leonard H. Goldenson, ABC, March 25, 1971.
34. Brief of DNC, Democratic National Committee v. FCC, 460 F. 2d 891 (D.C. Cir. 1971), *cert. den.,* 93 S.Ct. 42 (1972).
35. Letter from Corydon B. Dunham, NBC, to DNC, March 30, 1971.
36. Telegram from DNC to ABC, CBS, and NBC, April 8, 1971.
37. *Public Papers of the Presidents of the United States, Richard Nixon, 1971* (Washington, D.C.: Government Printing Office, 1972), p. 523.
38. Telegram from Corydon B. Dunham, NBC, to Joseph Califano, Jr., April 12, 1971.
39. Telegram from Elmer B. Lower, ABC, to DNC, April 9, 1971.
40. Letter from Sen. Robert Dole, RNC, to Leonard H. Goldenson, ABC, April 23, 1971.
41. Letter from Leonard H. Goldenson, ABC, to RNC, April 20, 1971.
42. Letter from RNC to William B. Ray, FCC, May 12, 1971.
43. *Democratic National Committee,* 31 FCC 2d 708 (1971).
44. Letter from DNC to William B. Ray, FCC, April 13, 1971.
45. *Democratic National Committee,* 31 FCC 2d 708 (1971).
46. Democratic National Committee Newsletter, December 1971.
47. *Democratic National Committee* v. *FCC* 460 F. 2d 891 (D.C. Cir. 1972), cert. den., 93 S.Ct. 42 (1972).
48. *Democratic National Committee,* 33 FCC 2d 631 (1972).
49. *Democratic National Committee,* 34 FCC 2d 572 (1972).
50. *Notice of Inquiry,* Docket No. 19260 (FCC 71-623, June 11, 1971).
51. First Report, Docket No. 19260, 36 FCC 2d 40 (1972).
52. Donald Meiklejohn, *Political Freedom: The Constitutional Powers of the People* (1960), p. 26, quoted in Brief for Intervenor, Columbia Broadcasting System, Inc., Democratic National Committee v. FCC, 450 F. 2d 642 (D.C. Cir. 1971).
53. Letter from CBS to William B. Ray, FCC, June 22, 1970, pp. 3–4.
54. Interview with W. Theodore Pierson, Sr., Washington, D.C., October 7, 1971.
55. Interview with Rep. Torbert H. Macdonald (D–Mass.), Washington, D.C., September 29, 1971.
56. O'Brien, "Television Is Threatening Our Democratic Processes," pp. 8, 9.
57. *Washington Star-News,* November 7, 1972.
58. John Stuart Mill, "On Liberty," quoted in *Red Lion Broadcasting Co.* v. *FCC,* 395 U.S. 367, 392 n. 19 (1969).
59. FCC News Release, April 7, 1971.
60. FCC News Release, November 10, 1972.
61. *Broadcasting,* September 14, 1970, p. 21.
62. *CATV,* June 21, 1971, p. 13.

63. Remarks by Clay T. Whitehead, Alfred I. DuPont–Columbia University Awards, Columbia University, New York, December 16, 1970.

64. Statement at ceremonies launching Public Broadcasting Service, September 28, 1970.

65. A. J. Liebling, *The Press* (New York: Ballantine Books, 1961), pp. 9–10.

66. "The Marketplace of Ideas: Would It Really Work Better If Access Were Controlled?" Remarks by Richard W. Jencks before the Federal Communications Bar Association, June 16, 1971.

67. *National Broadcasting Company* (WNBC), 16 FCC 2d 947 (1969).

68. Address by Frank Stanton, president of CBS, to the 1970 National Broadcast Editorial Conference, Park City, Utah, July 10, 1970.

69. RNC Letter to William B. Ray, FCC, May 12, 1971.

70. The British have recently established a right of opposition response to some broadcasts by government officials. As described by the 1970 *BBC Handbook,* ministerial broadcasts fall into two categories: "The first category relates to Ministers wishing to explain legislation or administrative policies approved by Parliament, or to seek the cooperation of the public in matters where there is a general consensus of opinion. . . . The second category relates to more important and normally infrequent occasions, when the Prime Minister or one of his senior Cabinet colleagues designated by him wishes to broadcast to the nation in order to provide information or explanation of events of prime national or international importance, or to seek the cooperation of the public in connection with these events" (British Broadcasting Company, *BBC Handbook 1970,* p. 87). The major opposition party has the right of reply to broadcasts in the second category. If it exercises this right, the system provides for a third broadcast, in which one man from the government and one from each of the two opposition parties debate the issue raised by the original ministerial broadcast.

But in Britain the opposition party functions as a shadow government, with a defined leader and position, and must take a position on all controversial issues before the government. In the American political system, the opposition party performs largely by running candidates against those of the party in power.

71. Congress took a first step toward reform in this direction in 1971 when it established by law a new presidential election campaign fund from which major party candidates for the presidency may draw an amount equal to fifteen cents per voter; minor party candidates may draw a proportionately lesser amount. The fund is financed by taxpayers, who may designate on their annual tax returns a one dollar contribution to the party of their choice or to a general account. These provisions will become effective for the first time in the presidential campaign of 1976. The fund is expected to diminish the financial burden of campaign broadcasting.

Meanwhile, on April 7, 1972, the new Federal Election Campaign Act of 1971 became effective. Subject to increases from inflation, the act limits communications media spending by candidates for federal office to ten cents per eligible voter (or $50,000 if greater); only six cents per voter can be spent on the broadcast media. Broadcasters are required to charge candidates their lowest unit rate for campaign advertising time. The FCC is given power to revoke broadcast licenses for failure to allow candidates reasonable access or to permit the purchase of reasonable amounts of broadcast time by a candidate.

CHAPTER 6
The Future of the Forum

1. Max Lerner, "Television: The Fourth Branch of Government," *TV Guide*, November 28, 1970, pp. 6, 7.
2. Richard Neustadt, *Presidential Power* (New York: John Wiley & Sons, Inc., 1960), p. 90.
3. Letter from Democratic National Committee to William B. Ray, Federal Communications Commission, April 13, 1971.
4. Brief for Intervenor, Republican National Committee, *Columbia Broadcasting System, Inc.,* v. *FCC,* 454 F. 2d 1018 (D.C. Cir. 1971).
5. Address by Frank Stanton, president of CBS, to the 1970 National Broadcast Editorial Conference, Park City, Utah, July 10, 1970.
6. Interview with Murray Chotiner, Washington, D.C., August 18, 1971.
7. Address by Frank Stanton, July 10, 1970.
8. This additional access would be expensive, of course, and all users might have to solicit funds during their broadcasts to pay for the broadcasts. The public, therefore, would control access to some extent by support for or rejection of the positions offered in the broadcasts. Even those groups or individuals who might not have to depend upon public solicitations are unlikely to purchase expensive broadcast time if no one is listening or watching.
9. Ben H. Bagdikian, *The Information Machines* (New York: Harper & Row, Publishers, 1971), p. 45.

APPENDIX C
Proposed Voters' Time Legislation

1. This bill was introduced as H.R. 14804 in the 92d Congress by Congressman Thomas O'Neill (D–Mass.). No action was taken on Rep. O'Neill's proposal.

SELECTED
BIBLIOGRAPHY

Books

Bagdikian, Ben H. *The Information Machines: Their Impact on Men and the Media.* New York: Harper & Row, Publishers, 1971.
Barnouw, Erik. *A Tower in Babel: A History of Broadcasting in the United States to 1933.* New York: Oxford University Press, 1966.
————. *The Golden Web: A History of Broadcasting in the United States, 1933–53.* New York: Oxford University Press, 1968.
————. *The Image Empire: A History of Broadcasting in the United States from 1953.* New York: Oxford University Press, 1970.
Barrett, Marvin, ed. *Survey of Broadcast Journalism 1969–1970.* New York: Grosset & Dunlap, 1970.
————, ed. *Survey of Broadcast Journalism 1970–1971.* New York: Grosset & Dunlap, 1971.
Chester, Edward W. *Radio, Television and American Politics.* New York: Sheed & Ward, 1969.
Cornwell, Elmer E., Jr. *Presidential Leadership of Public Opinion.* Bloomington: Indiana University Press, 1965.

Johnson, Nicholas. *How to Talk Back to Your Television Set.* New York: Bantam Books, 1970.

Lee, Richard W., ed. *Politics and the Press.* Washington, D.C.: Acropolis Books, 1970.

McGinniss, Joe. *The Selling of the President 1968.* New York: Simon & Schuster, Pocket Books, 1970.

MacNeil, Robert. *The People Machine.* New York: Harper & Row, Publishers, 1968.

Mayer, Martin. *About Television.* New York: Harper & Row, Publishers, 1972.

Mickelson, Sig. *The Electric Mirror: Politics in an Age of Television.* New York: Dodd, Mead & Co., 1972.

New York Times. *The Mass Media and Politics.* New York: Arno Press, 1972.

Reston, James. *The Artillery of the Press: Its Influence on American Foreign Policy.* New York: Harper & Row, Publishers, Colophon Books, 1967.

Rubin, Bernard. *Political Television.* Belmont, Calif.: Wadsworth Publishing Co., 1967.

Small, William. *To Kill a Messenger: Television News and the Real World.* New York: Hastings House, 1970.

Thomson, Charles A. H. *Television and Presidential Politics.* Washington, D.C.: Brookings Institution, 1956.

The Twentieth Century Fund Commission on Campaign Costs in the Electronic Era. *Voters' Time.* New York: The Twentieth Century Fund, 1969.

Whale, John. *The Half-Shut Eye: Television and Politics in Britain and America.* London: Macmillan & Co., 1969.

Articles and Miscellaneous Material

Becker, Samuel L. "Presidential Power: The Influence of Broadcasting." *Quarterly Journal of Speech* 47 (February 1961): 10–18.

Goldschlager, Seth. "The Supreme Court and the Media: The Reporters and the Reported." Senior thesis, Yale University Law School, 1971.

Hearings on the Fairness Doctrine before the Special Subcommittee on Investigations of the House Committee on Interstate and Foreign Commerce, 90th Cong., 2d sess., ser. no. 90–33 (1968).

Hearings on S.J. Res. 209 before the Communications Subcommittee of the Senate Committee on Commerce, 91st Cong., 2d sess., ser. no. 91–74 (1970).

Lerner, Max. "The Fourth Branch of Government." *TV Guide,* September 28, 1970.
O'Brien, Lawrence F. "Television Is Threatening Our Democratic Process." *TV Guide,* September 19, 1970.
Stanton, Frank. Address to the 1970 National Broadcast Editorial Conference, Park City, Utah, July 10, 1970.
Comment, "Televised Presidential Addresses and the FCC's Fairness Doctrine." *Columbia Journal of Law and Social Problems* 7 (1971): 75.

INDEX